SETTING HEARTS ON FIRE

Come, Holy Spirit,
Fill the hearts of your people;
Kindle in us the fire of your love.
Send forth your Spirit,
And we shall be created,
And you will renew the face of the earth.
Amen.

SETTING HEARTS ON FIRE
A Spirituality for Leaders

Sister Patricia Sullivan, RSM and
Reverend Timothy Brown, SJ

ALBA·HOUSE NEW·YORK

SOCIETY OF ST. PAUL, 2187 VICTORY BLVD., STATEN ISLAND, NEW YORK 10314

ST PAULS

Scripture passages from *The New Testament and Psalms*, Catholic edition, translated from the original Greek and Hebrew by Mark A. Wauck and Miguel Miguens. Copyright 1997, Society of St. Paul. All rights reserved. Used with permission.

Library of Congress Cataloging-in-Publication Data

   Sullivan, Patricia, Sister.
     Setting hearts on fire: a spirituality for leaders / Patricia Sullivan
   and Timothy Brown.
       p.   cm.
     Includes bibliographical references.
     ISBN 0-8189-0771-1
     1. Leadership — Religious aspects — Christianity. 2. Christian
   leadership. I. Brown, Timothy, Reverend. II. Title.
   BV4597.53.L43S85   1997
   248.8'92 — dc21   96-50064
                                    CIP

Produced and designed in the United States of America by the
Fathers and Brothers of the Society of St. Paul,
2187 Victory Boulevard, Staten Island, New York 10314,
as part of their communications apostolate.

ISBN: 0-8189-0771-1

Printing Information:

Current Printing - first digit   1   2   3   4   5   6   7   8   9   10

Year of Current Printing - first year shown

1997   1998   1999   2000   2001   2002   2003   2004   2005

Table of Contents

Calling Upon the Spirit

God's Spirit joins with our spirit, alleluia!
To declare that we are children of God, alleluia!

Holy Spirit, Creator! In the beginning you moved over the waters,
and from your breath all creatures first drew their life.
Holy Spirit, come!

Holy Spirit, Counselor! By your inspiration
the people of God and the prophets spoke and acted in faith.
You clothed them in your power,
to be the bearers of your Word.
Holy Spirit, come!

Holy Spirit, Life-giver! You overshadowed the Virgin Mary
to make her the mother of the Son of God.
Holy Spirit, come!

Holy Spirit, Sanctifier! By you, Jesus grew in wisdom and grace.
On the day of his baptism, you descended on him as a dove
to consecrate him and fill him with power
to bear witness to the Father.
Holy Spirit, come!

Holy Spirit, Empowered! By you, the disciples left all
at Jesus' call and followed him,
proclaiming the glories of his Name
to the ends of the earth!
Holy Spirit, come!

Father, in your infinite goodness, set us aflame
with that fire of the Spirit Christ brought upon the earth
and longed to see ablaze,
for he lives and reigns with you and the Spirit now and forever.
Amen.

— from *Praise God: Common Prayer at Taizé*

The Spirit Song

Refrain: Come Holy Spirit take hold of my life, lead me in your
perfect love.
Teach me your ways, enlighten my heart, lead me home.
Spirit of wisdom take hold of my heart...

Introduction

Why Another Book on Leadership?

Over the last few years there has been a trend for organizations in search of higher profits and productivity and better leadership to jump from one leadership theory to the next — spawning an entire industry of management consultants and textbooks. Organizations have moved from extending the "Glad Hand of Human Relations" in the 1950's to the more recent "One Minute Manager," who while leading a work-force of people in search of excellence are cultivating the seven habits most often found in highly effective people. What makes a good leader? And what makes a good leader great? Experts have analyzed management and leadership styles from the autocratic to the participative. And the best-seller lists tout books selling in the hundreds of thousands on leaders and the leadership styles of charismatic and highly successful individuals — the Sam Walton's and Lee Iacocca's of America.

The evolving portrait or theory of the successful organizational leader increasingly recognizes that these individuals hold values like respect for the dignity of people, the importance of dialogue and inclusion, and work as a value in itself. Today's new leader *empowers* (a great new corporate buzzword!) people and makes work "fun." These leaders know how to inspire and "set people on fire." It's interesting to note, too, that these values have been around for a long time: traditionally, as Judeo-Christian or spiritual values.

But curiously absent in all of the discussion of what makes a good leader and what leadership theories succeed has been an analysis of the leadership style of one great leader — a person whose life and example spawned an enduring institution spanning twenty centuries; someone who garnered more loyal followers than any other and who, like Sam Walton, started dirt poor with a lowly background, but who knew how to inherit the earth; a leader whose charisma and philosophy caused the true "culture change" and revolution so many organizational — if not societal — leaders seek today; and who, beyond the wildest dreams of today's leaders, was able to show those who followed him that he cared deeply for them and not just for what they could do for the "bottom line."

While organizational leaders are eager to talk of "team spirit," or changing corporate culture — the very spirit of the organization — few have taken the time to address the spiritual side of leading, or more specifically, their own spirituality. Leaders who *inspire* are at a premium in recruiting circles, and yet no one can precisely define what this means. In many corporate and public circles, discussions of faith and spirituality are sometimes seen as something of an embarrassment — despite overwhelming statistical and anecdotal evidence that Americans, young and old alike, are perhaps the most religious people on earth. The authors of this book suggest that individual spirituality is a crucial part of leading and that a spiritual model for leading can be successfully woven with modern leadership theory and practice.

Some readers might feel uncomfortable with the term "spirituality." It's a nebulous term in a world full of exacting, concrete requirements. "You mean that religious stuff?" some might ask. "I go to Church every Sunday. We are involved in the community. I'm a good person. I think I've got that covered." But being a member of a faith tradition or practicing a particular religion is not what is meant by spirituality. Spirituality transcends the particular faith one subscribes to. It has more to do with moving inward to examine the core values — the moral commitments one holds — and to care for the soul. Thomas Moore says that in our spirituality, we reach for consciousness, awareness, and the highest values. "In the broadest sense," Moore writes, "spirituality is an aspect of any attempt to approach or attend to the invisible factors in life and to transcend the personal, concrete, finite particulars of this world; [they] are of the soul and attending to the soul's needs are crucial to leaders, yet often overlooked."

The fundamental source of being human is spirituality — an awareness of God's Spirit in one's life. Spirituality involves being aware of relationships with others, with thoughts, words and actions. It controls beliefs, attitudes and practices by which people give witness to Christ and acknowledge God in their lives.

In illustrating that good ethical behavior comes from the soul, Kenneth Blanchard and Norman Vincent Peale tell the thought-provoking parable of "The Lost Soul." It seems that a vice president (VP) began to search for his soul in response to an employee he'd fired who told him he hoped he'd find his soul again. The VP reports his soul to the Lost and Found Department, which refers him to the security officer, a specialist in soul recovery. The "soul specialist" suggests that the VP go with him to the president and ask him if he has seen his lost soul. The president blurts out, "What on earth would I want with a soul? Competition in business is too tough for souls, they get in the way of clear thinking. By the way, make sure the figures come out right in your presentation to the corporate people."

The VP and the security officer leave the president's office. The VP still wants to find his soul, and an inter-office memo is sent out asking if any employees can recall seeing his soul in action.

One employee comes forward and tells the VP of his gratitude to him when he reported hitting his car in the parking garage. Through honesty the VP gets his soul back.

The moral of this parable is that the soul is where you have your values, your purpose in life, and the picture of the kind of person you want to be. And in any organization, the soul should be represented by the top leaders and managers through their hope, vision, and purpose for the organization. Yet it often isn't, because people just don't take the time — or see the need — to turn inward and attend to the soul.

But in this busy world, how can one possibly take the time to turn inward? What, some readers might question, can that possibly do for me as a leader? In "Leading From Within," Parker Palmer says that part of the problem is that "people rise to leadership in our society by a tendency toward extroversion, which means a tendency to ignore what is going on inside themselves." By doing so, they come to "regard the inner life as illusory." By denying their inner life, they deny their own spirituality. Palmer says that this doesn't have to be the case "if we have education for leadership that is not simply about the skills to manipulate the external world, but is also about the personal and corporate disciplines of the inner world."

Vaclev Havel says that "the salvation of this world lies nowhere else than in the human heart." And there is an old saying: "To change the outside, you must first change the inside." John W. Gardner in his book, *On Leadership* (p. 90), says that the first step to becoming a better leader is not actions, it is understanding. The first question is how to think about leadership. Action follows *after* understanding. And understanding can only occur by taking the time for inward reflection, by making the inner journey. Perhaps by taking time to reflect upon one's leadership style and a spiritual dimension to leading, leaders will find deep sources of freedom and power to effect changes they never dreamed possible.

Jesus Christ was perhaps the greatest leader of all time. What made him a great leader? And what does reflecting upon Jesus' leadership model offer to today's leader?

Setting Hearts on Fire: A Spirituality for Leaders looks at Jesus as leader — a leader who knew how to shape a vision, dialogue with people, provide hope, and offer the possibility for transformation. It also relates popular models of leadership to spiritual aspects of leading, finding ways that the two can converge and strengthen one another, creating a unique fit for leaders seeking to reconcile numerous organizational management models which too often seem to have no place for spiritual values. Each chapter of this book examines a specific aspect of Jesus as the ultimate spiritual leader and relates it to today's leader. Prayers for reflection and questions for discussion follow.

The Great Leader: Is There A Formula?

In 1959, Warren Bennis, a leading expert on leadership, claimed that "of all the hazy and confounding areas in social psychology, leadership theory undoubtedly contends for the top nomination. And, ironically, probably more has been written and less known about leadership than about any other topic in the behavioral sciences." Filley, House, and Kerr, in their extensive research in 1976, once again highlight the confusing and contradictory nature of the literature associated with leadership. These critics found that the so-called "Great Man" and "Great Woman" propositions, behavioral approaches, and situational theories of leadership were oversimplified. No single trait, no single behavior, no situational fit between a leader's traits and behavior was found to be associated with effective leadership that results in raising subordinates' satisfaction and performance. In other words, this research found no recipe, no cookbook, no formula or characteristics that would predict greatness in a leader.

Still, a plethora of pragmatists, theorists, and researchers continue to put their observations, theories, and findings into models of behavior that direct and inspire many leaders in a variety of governmental, business, and religious institutions. Somewhat surprisingly, none of these models or philosophies give emphasis to the importance of a religious source or a spiritual commitment in being a good leader. Yet the spiritual connection is decidedly present in shaping corporation decisions:

> Religious values [temper] an organization's single-minded pursuit of its own good and the single-minded pursuit of self-interest. Religious values lead people to rebel at the enforced unemployment of millions, challenge a culture which denies responsibility to the persons doing the work, and reach out to make meaningful the Proverb's plea: "Let not loyalty and

faithfulness forsake you." *(Harvard Divinity Bulletin*, Feb-March, 1984:4-7)

Even before Christ's time, the value of spiritual awareness for leaders was recognized by people like Lao Tzu, the great Chinese sage of the 6th century B.C. In Tao Te Ching, a text on how to rule a kingdom and to be a wise leader, he wrote that spiritual awareness characterizes the leader who knows how things happen — and how to make things happen:

> Group work must include spiritual awareness, if it is to touch the existential anxiety of our times. Without awe, the awful remains unspoken; a diffuse malaise remains.
>
> Be willing to speak of traditional religion, no matter how offended some groups or members may be. Overcome the bias against the word "God." The great force of our spiritual roots lies in tradition, like it or not.
>
> The wise leader models spiritual behavior and lives in harmony with spiritual values. There is a way of knowing, higher than reason; there is a self, greater than egocentricity.

The leader demonstrates the power of selflessness and the unity of all creation. One modern example of this which touched people throughout the world was the meeting of three world leaders at Camp David in 1979. Menachim Begin (a Jew), Anwar Sadat (a Moslem), and Jimmy Carter (a Christian), each from his own spiritual convictions took action to bring peace between the Jewish and Arab worlds.

Current popular examples of literature on leadership seem to focus on naming structures and processes that affect leadership behavior positively or negatively. It seems that leaders are encouraged to inspire others by striking a balance between providing structures and allowing creative processes to work among groups or within organizations, in order for them to function effectively. Some popular best-sellers support this approach.

A Passion for Excellence: The Leadership Difference, the

1985 New York Times best-seller by Tom Peters and Nancy Austin, defines leadership as vision, cheerleading, enthusiasm, love, trust, verve, passion, obsession, consistency. Good leadership, they say, involves using symbols, paying attention to what's on one's calendar, having a flair for the dramatic, and finding a way to create heroes at all levels. It is also coaching effectively, wandering around, and educating. Peters and Austin view leadership as present at all levels of the organization and as depending on a million little things done with obsession, consistency and care. These million little things will amount to nothing, they argue, if vision and basic belief are absent.

Robert Wess offers another source of inspiration in his book, *Leadership Secrets of Attila the Hun*. This book is acclaimed as a "brilliant leadership masterpiece" and as "an imaginative and colorful approach to relating leadership principles that have long served those having the will to lead."

One of the best inspirational works on leadership is Max DePree's *Leadership is an Art* (1989). DePree, chairman and CEO of Herman Miller, Inc., a furniture maker, gives a wise message. He believes that leadership is not a science or discipline, but rather an art that is felt, experienced, and created. He argues that humanistic and Christian values are at the heart of artful leadership. Covenantal relationships, participative management, good design, and allegiance to a corporate value-system are among the practices of artful leadership. DePree left a legacy of leadership for leaders in any organizational setting. His book has since been acclaimed by leaders as "a design for success and for developing the generous spirit within ourselves" and as a "wisdom book for our times." Perhaps it is no surprise that DePree's company was chosen by *Fortune* magazine as one of the 100 best companies to work for in America.

In spite of the "ideal" models available to inspire leaders, leadership today is characterized by a lack of commitment and by lapses in ethics. The leadership environment is tainted at the international, national, and organizational levels in private and public enterprise.

Corruption and turnover are rampant in U.S. organizations. *New York Times* columnist and author Anna Quindlen writes that despite pleas for a "kinder, gentler nation,"

> ... we have the sour disposition of a country with diminished expectations, a country whose people have been living through a depression both economic and spiritual... It is a depression our government refuses to acknowledge, so the American people live with a sinking feeling that their sinking standard of living is a failure of the individual. "I really don't feel as if politicians have any connection to me personally," a college student told me. Our elections are as big, bright and empty as balloons. *(Thinking Out Loud*, p. 55)

We are a nation and a world in search of real leaders. We have lost a sense of meaning in politics, and many workers, now more than ever, have lost a sense of having real leadership. There exists a desperate need for those in business, government, and religion to develop their leadership potential by pursuing a meaningful personal and organizational life and by working toward a just society.

But Christian men and women find that it is not easy to articulate a leadership model when they are struggling to balance an authentic Christian life with a professional life in a world characterized by self-gratification, self-fulfillment and intolerance; where the poor, minorities and other powerless groups are virtually invisible; and where, all too often, the standard for success in business is profit, the bottom line, and, following a philosophy such as the one advocated by a popular bumper sticker, "He who has the most toys in the end — WINS!"

How can Christians assume a leadership style that is based on the Gospel message? How can we translate what we espouse as an authentic Christian life into practical and compassionate leadership that truly reflects our commitment to Christ? Living out a spiritual model of leadership may take different forms and, depending upon the individual, may manifest itself to varying degrees. If it is truly the spark from within, a tour of one's own heart that leads to becoming a better leader, how do you measure the stirrings of the heart? These questions are difficult to answer. But the premise of this book is that it is God's grace and the power of the Holy Spirit that truly underlie the extent of each leader's influence.

In this book we attempt to reflect on leadership models in light of the Christian spirit of leadership. We contend that the secular and spiritual dimensions converge and can be captured by anyone, taught to everyone, and denied to no one. We believe that the quest for balancing the secular and the spiritual dimensions of leadership can be learned and translated into action in a model where L-E-A-D-E-R-S-H-I-P is used as an acronym. Perhaps some pragmatism will bring the spirit needed for effective — and reflective — leadership into the practical world of daily action in which we all live.

By reflecting on secular leadership models along with analysis and reflection on Christ's leadership style, Christian leaders can grow in their interior peace and can be pillars of stability and calm in shaping and living the organizational life of the 1990s and into the next millennium.

A leadership model that encompasses spiritual and secular aspects seems appropriate for Christian leaders who are challenged to live Christ's dictum to the apostles: "Behold, I am sending you off like sheep among wolves; be as wise as serpents and as guileless as doves" (Mt 10:16). In confronting the pressures, competition, and power struggles of the secular world, Christian leaders need to remember that Christ's spirit pervades the world in subtle and explicit ways. We find in Mark 8:14-21 a key Gospel passage that exemplifies that spirit:

> Now they had forgotten to bring bread, and except for one loaf they had none with them in the boat. [Jesus] was instructing them and saying, "Take care! Watch out for the leaven of the Pharisees and the leaven of Herod!" but they kept arguing among themselves because they didn't have bread. Realizing this, he said to them, "Why are you arguing because you don't have bread? Do you still neither see nor understand? Do *you* have hardened hearts? *Can't you see* with your eyes? *Can't you hear* with your ears? *Don't you remember* when I

broke the five loaves for the five thousand, how many bas-
kets full of leftovers you picked up?" "Twelve," they said.
"And the seven for the four thousand, how many large bas-
kets full of leftovers did you pick up?" "Seven," they said.
Then he said to them, "Don't you understand yet?"

St. Ignatius Loyola in *The Spiritual Exercises* teaches that our perceptions of Christ's leadership can be enhanced by using our senses.
If you desire to imitate Christ's leadership, he says, recommend
yourself to the Divine Majesty. Contemplate seeing, hearing, smell-
ing, touching, tasting, and being open to the spirit of Christ. This
involves trying to bring the whole of your being into the vividness
of this experience. David Fleming, S.J., in *The Spiritual Exercises
of St. Ignatius Loyola*, elaborates upon this concept:

> In many ways, this setting is the most passive prayer experi-
> ence; it is not a matter of thinking new thoughts or even of
> looking for new images... It is akin to the passive way my
> senses take in sights, smells, sounds, and feelings as the au-
> tomatic datum for my attention.

Prayerfully applying one's senses is only one way to attempt to
weave secular and spiritual dimensions of leadership. A reflective
reading through the following chapters may assist the reader in
gaining some insight into the spirit of Christ's leadership. It might
also be useful to keep these questions in mind: *What kind of leader
was Christ? What was his leadership style? How did he act in situations that demanded his leadership?*

This book's contemplative approach makes its content different from any other of the scores of books written about leadership,
management styles, and organizational behavior. Each chapter
contains several examples from popular cultural concepts of leadership and attempts to illuminate — and to add a new dimension
to — them with scriptural passages, stories, and prayers. Each chapter begins with a prayer to the Holy Spirit and closes with a psalm,
which is intended to help readers invoke Christ's spirit into the
reading.

As mentioned previously, applying our senses (in meditation or contemplation) is just one way of praying in imitation of Christ. Ignatius suggests that we bring all our faculties — intellect, emotions, imagination, and desires — together in prayer. By letting ourselves go and taking on the mind, the heart, and the spirit of Christ, we immerse ourselves physically and spiritually in the mystery of his life and his example that we attempt to contemplate. This form of prayer brings us beyond a mere intellectual appreciation of the meaning of Christ's teachings and way of life. By bringing all of ourselves into this experience, we can adopt aspects of Christ's leadership style, and can better adapt this style to our working and living situation.

Christ challenges us to open our eyes and ears to the possibility — ever present in every day, perhaps in a "million little things" — of ushering the Kingdom of God into our world. This challenge is difficult today. We are overloaded with information systems but are unable to process, sift, and reflect upon the hoard of information bombarding us. We have access to a multitude of communication networks, and yet more than ever we have trouble truly listening, truly communicating. We find the pace of life accelerating, without finding the time to sit back and ask, "What does all of this mean?" By neglecting to step back to reflect, and to see Christ's spirit continually working today in our world, we miss one vital fact: Christ is a living model of leadership for us through his spirit.

Origen described Christ in a way that should guide our own way of proceeding as leaders in the world:

> Christ is the source; the stream of living water flows out of him. He is the bread and gives life. And thus he is spikenard and gives fragrance, ointment which transforms us into the anointed. He is something for each particular sense of the soul. He is called Light, so that the soul might have eyes. Word, so that it might have ears to hear. Bread, so that it might savor him. Oil of anointing, so that it might breathe in the fragrance of the word. And he has become flesh, so that the inward hand

of the soul might be able to touch something of the Word of life, which fashions itself to correspond with the various manifestations of prayer and which leaves no sense of the soul untouched by his grace.

The leadership model presented in this book may not be new to many readers. In fact, we hope that it is not! We suggest looking at the concepts from a different perspective, from a Christian focus, to capture the spirit of Christ. Each reader may view the readings from his or her experience. Each, we hope, will perhaps see his or her style of leadership mirrored in some of what is here. We believe that everyone is called to be a leader in some form. It is the spirit in which that leadership manifests itself that is unique to each person.

Francois Mauriac writes:

And when Jesus tore himself from the midst of his disciples, ascended, and was dissolved in light, it was no final departure. Already he was lying in ambush at the turn of the road which went from Jerusalem to Damascus, watching for Saul, his beloved persecutor.

Thenceforth in the destiny of everyone there was to be this God who lies in wait.

Perhaps a prayer may help you to capture the spirit of Christ's leadership that lies in wait to be manifested more fully in your life and in the lives of those around you:

Glory be to God our Creator,
to Jesus the Christ,
and to the Holy Spirit who dwells in our midst,
both now and forever. Amen.

Timothy Brown, SJ
Patricia Sullivan, RSM

Spirit Leading

The Spirit of God rests upon me,
The Spirit of God consecrates me,
The Spirit of God bids me go forth
to proclaim God's peace and joy.

The Spirit of God sends me forth,
Called to witness the kingdom of Christ among all nations;
Called to proclaim the good news of Christ to the poor.
Called to console the hearts overcome with great sorrow.
Called to comfort the poor who mourn and who weep.
Called to announce the grace of salvation to all.
Called to reveal the glory among all the people.

My spirit rejoices in God, my Savior.

Based on Isaiah 61:1-2; Luke 4:18-19
Lucien Deiss, C.S.Sp., b. 1920
Word Library Pub. Inc., 1970
Used with permission.

SETTING HEARTS ON FIRE

Chapter One

Leadership

"Would you tell me, please, which way I ought to go from
   here?"
"That depends a good deal on where you want to get to,"
   said the Cat.
"I don't much care where —" said Alice.
"Then it doesn't matter which way you go," said the Cat.
"— so long as I get *somewhere*," Alice added as an
   explanation.
"Oh, you're sure to do that," said the Cat, "if you only
   walk long enough."

　　　　　　　　—Lewis Carroll, *Alice's Adventures in Wonderland*

Only when we know what we're made of and what we
   want to make of it can we begin our lives.

　　　　　　　　—Warren Bennis, *Leadership*

LEADERSHIP: THE SPIRITUAL MODEL

Leading and Managing: What's the Difference?

Perhaps you are familiar with this vignette from Lewis Carroll's *Alice's Adventures in Wonderland*:

> "Would you tell me, please, which way I ought to go from here?"
> "That depends a good deal on where you want to get to,"
>   said the Cat.
> "I don't much care where —" said Alice.
> "Then it doesn't matter which way you go," said the Cat.
> "— so long as I get *somewhere*," Alice added as an explanation.
> "Oh, you're sure to do that," said the Cat, "if you only walk long
>   enough."

As the discourse between Alice and the Cat shows, Alice is clearly without a goal or vision. Alice is lacking one of the qualities unique to good leaders: Leaders have the imagination in defining and shaping a direction or vision.

Leadership can be said to be the capacity to influence a group toward the achievement of goals or the ability to move followers to realize a vision and objectives held by the leader or shared by the leader and his or her followers. The source of this influence might be informal or formal in the business, government, and countless other groups and organizations that shape the world in which we live, work, and play. Richard Johnson writes in *Quality Progress* magazine, "Leadership is the act of taking people somewhere with an idea — visioning them into the future and then taking them there... Successful leadership depends on the ability to create a vision that is then 'painted' for people in terms of the benefits they will experience."

Leadership and management are two distinct yet complementary systems of action. While leadership is more often associated with having a vision and coping with change, and managership is associated more with dealing with complex situations, both leadership and managership involve planning, organizing, leading, and

3

evaluating in light of an organization's mission, goals, and objectives.

In discussing the distinctions many writers on leadership so carefully draw between leaders and managers, John Gardner writes that:

> In the process leaders generally end up looking like a cross between Napoleon and the Pied Piper and managers like unimaginative clods. This troubles me.... Even the most visionary leader is faced on occasion with decisions that every manager faces. (*On Leadership*, p. 4)

Gardner (*ibid.*) says that leaders and leader/managers distinguish themselves from the general run of managers in at least six ways:

1. They think longer term — beyond the day's crises, beyond the quarterly report, beyond the horizon.

2. In thinking about the unit they are heading, they grasp its relationship to larger realities — the larger organization of which they are a part, conditions external to the organization, global trends.

3. They reach and influence constituents beyond their jurisdictions, beyond boundaries, enabling them to bind together the fragmented constituencies that must work together to solve a problem.

4. They put heavy emphasis on the intangibles of *vision*, *values*, and *motivation* and understand intuitively the non-rational and unconscious elements in leader-constituent interaction.

5. They have the political skill to cope with the conflicting requirements of multiple constituencies.

6. They think in terms of renewal. The routine manager tends to accept organizational structure and process as it exists.

The leader or leader/manager seeks the revisions of process and structure required by ever-changing reality.

Formal managerial or leadership roles do not guarantee effective leadership. And power or status do not necessarily make one a good leader. Effective leadership means the ability to get the most from people, whether through formal or informal authority sources. An appointed manager, administrator, or leader may be good at producing consistently good results and meeting deadlines and objectives. This "good manager", however, fails as a leader if followers have not been inspired. The art or spirit of leadership involves influencing, guiding, and directing others to new heights of understanding, interacting, and commitment. Thus, the difference between a leader and a manager lies in the ability to motivate or inspire others — in other words, *to give a vision.*

Leadership is not measured by merely examining the quality of the leader but by reading the signs among the followers. Leadership expert Max DePree asks: "Are followers reaching their potential? Are they learning? Serving? Do they achieve the required results? Do they change with grace? Manage conflict?" (*Leadership is an Art*, p. 10) John Gardner says that the important question is not whether the followers believe in the leaders — although this is important — but whether leaders believe in their followers.

Practically speaking, a "good leader" needs to be a "good manager" and a "good manager" needs to be a "good leader." It seems reasonable to assume that a balance of leadership and managership is essential to personal and organizational satisfaction, productivity, and influence.

Professor Abraham Zaleznik of the Harvard Business School argues that leaders and managers are different kinds of people. He says that leaders and managers have different personalities and orientations toward goals, work, human relations, and themselves. The table below summarizes Zaleznik's contrast between leaders and managers.

Table 1

	MANAGERS	LEADERS
PERSONALITY	Persistent	Visionary
	Tough-minded	Creates Excitement
	Analytical	Presence may undermine development of managers
	Problem solver	
	Tolerant	
	Instinct for survival	
GOALS	Supports goals and purposes of the organization	Acts instead of reacts to goals
	Takes systematic steps to reach goals	Shapes ideas
	Uses collective experience to get where going	Takes active and personal role toward goals
	Adopts impersonal attitudes toward goals	Asks to change way people think about what is possible, desirable, necessary
WORK	Approaches work problems conservatively	Develops fresh approaches to long-standing problems
	Seeks more mundane, practical work and uses rewards and punishment	Open to new options to resolve issues
	Limits creative or ethical behavior in guiding destinies of corporate enterprise.	
HUMAN RELATIONS	Prefers to work with people and avoid solitary activity	Does not mind solitude
	Perpetuates group conflicts through decreased ability to communicate	Uses power to influence thoughts and actions of others
	Relates to people based on role in decision making	Relates to people with inner perceptiveness. Establishes and breaks off intense one-on-one relationships
	Stems from strengthening the institution	Feels separate from the environment
		Works in organization but never belongs
		Fosters culture of individualism, possibly elitism

Zaleznik's model may be viewed as a reflection of the hard-line, stern quality of law (an autocratic management model) and the call of Christ for a way of love (a leadership model). Christ called for a new vision to replace the old vision of life. Christ demonstrated single-hearted relations with God and with God's people. Christ as a leader managed his life and ministry in terms of his Father's will. He transcended power, popularity, influence, glory, money, titles, and many other possessions that characterize managerial life. And yet he was arguably the most effective leader of all time — whose vision made a lasting contribution to humanity.

The Shadow Side of Leadership

If leaders are called to be just and to shape a vision for a better world, why, some people ask, do we see so many leaders who seem to thrive because their leadership style functions mostly through power, and embodies oppression, fear, dominance and other negatives? It is important at this point to acknowledge the shadow side of leadership — the dark face of leadership, which derives from negative spirituality.

We live in a time of political corruption, ethnic cleansing, corporate raiding, racism, gay-bashing, child pornography and violence. And, however well-intentioned, efforts of many of today's leaders seem to be ineffectual to combat these problems. Parker Palmer, in *Leading From Within*, says that leaders can project either light or conditions that are of the shadow, a spirit of hope or a spirit of despair. Most people could probably name a few modern leaders who obviously act out of and project the spirit of evil and despair. But because many people rise to leadership in society because of a tendency towards extroversion, this means they also may have a tendency to ignore or deny their inner life.

According to Palmer, this, in turn, means leaders may operate out of the dark side not because they mean to be evil, but simply because they find it easier to focus on manipulating the external world rather than making the much more difficult inner journey. One of the biggest shadows Palmer sees is that "inside a lot of leaders is deep insecurity about their own identity," which is especially "hard to see in extroverted people." This leads to their creating "institutional settings which *deprive* other people of *their* identity as a way of dealing with the unexamined fears in the leaders themselves." Palmer says that if you are ever with people who know "all the way down" who they are, whose identity doesn't depend on a role that might be taken away at any moment, you are with people and in settings that give you identity and *empower* you to be someone. This, he says, is a core issue in the spirituality for leadership.

Palmer says leaders operate out of other shadows, such as "the perception that the universe is essentially a hostile battleground," which in turn becomes a self-fulfilling prophecy; a "functional atheism," the belief that "ultimate responsibility for everything rests with me." This leads to workaholism, stress, unhealthy priorities, and to fear — of chaos which leads to an addiction to control and rigidity. Leaders can start recovering the power of the inner journey by realizing that the universe is working together for good, that ours is not the only act in town, and that creation comes out of chaos. Palmer argues that by making the inner journey, leaders do not have to *be* their fears, and they do not have to create a world in which those fears dominate the conditions of many people. Perhaps, instead, they can be leaders who cast light on the many troubling issues shadowing our world.

Creative and courageous expressions of a new vision of Christian life demand that managerial leaders show the positive face of leadership and defend against oppressive systems that give rise to homelessness, hunger, unjust wages, and poverty. These outcomes are consequences of the dark side of leadership and managerial styles that deny others their dignity, as results of leaders who organize to pass unjust laws or to oppress a group of people or even a whole country. Such things break the human spirit and cannot be healed by sacramental absolution alone. Christlike leadership demands that leaders be advocates for victims of violence or oppression in the workplace, the state, and the country.

This kind of leadership spirit, which leading managers or

managerial leaders seek, can be seen in Christ's reading of the prophet Isaiah's scroll:

> The spirit of the Lord is upon me,
> because he has anointed me
> to bring the good news to the poor.
> He has sent me to proclaim release to captives
> and recovery of sight to the blind,
> to set at liberty the oppressed,
> to proclaim the acceptable year of the Lord.
> When he had rolled up the scroll and handed it back to the attendant, he sat down; and the eyes of everyone in the synagogue were fixed on him. Then he began to tell them, "Today this Scripture has been fulfilled in your hearing." All the people... were amazed at the gracious words that came from his mouth. (Lk 4:18-22)

The gracious words of Christian leaders should be rooted in a true understanding of what it means to call ourselves Christians — adopting Christ's name, receiving Christ's body and blood, and believing that God does indeed live in us. Being a leader or manager of people is an honor and a responsibility. Just think! To influence lives, to have the chance to shape people — and perhaps larger circles around them — for the better. And so leaders and managers who seek the spiritual model of leadership are called to conform to Christ's person, who said that his food (his purpose) was to do the will of the One who sent him (Jn 4:34). Christ was both a leader (as in his vision and teachings, which inspired countless millions) and a manager (as with managing the hunger of crowds very practically — with loaves and fishes). As both leading manager and managerial leader, Christ knew when to stay with people and when to move on (Lk 4:42-44).

Curiously, modern managerial and leadership literature is beginning to recognize what have been traditionally seen as "Christian" virtues. Books like *The One Minute Manager* point out the importance of recognizing people and taking time to acknowledge them and praise them. The widely popular total quality management (TQM) revolution has, as its foundation, respect for people's dignity and learning to listen to and value their contributions — to establish true dialogue. Industrial psychologist James R. Fisher, Ph.D., is author of *Work Without Managers: A View From the Trenches.* He writes that "In my years as a corporate executive and then consultant, I've learned this: while technical systems change rapidly, the systems that govern our social behavior have evolved little in 2000 years. And we get what we want out of life only by working with and through others." Fisher wrote down some rules that read like a "Beatitudes for the Corporate World" that help him maintain that perspective.

Cynics may question whether these ideas are motivated by "the bottom line" or by a true desire to see every person as a worthwhile human being with unique dignity; for after all, they might ask, won't some be more productive if they feel they are a valued part of a team? But whether motivated by profit reasons or for prophet reasons, some of these leadership models are a positive development for many organizations. It seems that popular models for successful leading — and all the recipes for success, the guidelines and checklists that leaders and managers consume so voraciously — can be boiled down to this: *love others as you love yourself!*

In the evolution of modern leadership models, there seem to be close parallels with a Christlike model for leadership. In their personal and professional lives, leaders are called to care for one another as members of a loving family care for one another (Lk 15:11-32; 11:11-13). Those who look closely at Jesus' style of leading and managing can learn that God is loving and gentle and wants life for us. Leaders — and followers — are expected to love one another as they have been loved (Jn 15:12).

Peter's First Letter to God's chosen people captures the Christian spirit of leadership: "Each one, as a good manager of God's different gifts, must use for the good of others the special gift he has received from God. Whoever preaches must preach God's messages; whoever serves must serve with the strength that God gives him, so that in all things praise may be given to God through

Jesus Christ, to whom belong glory and power forever and ever. Amen" (1 P 4:10-11, *Good News Bible*).

As Christ's followers, Christian leaders acknowledge Christ as "supreme over every spiritual ruler and authority" (Col 2:10). They acknowledge that the kingdom of God does not mean authority over food and drink (or work forces or bottom lines!), but "righteousness, peace, and joy which the Holy Spirit gives." Christian leaders must pursue whatever creates peace and mutual understanding (Rm 14:17-19).

Spiritual Reflection

Take a moment to reflect upon the following prayer. Find a quiet place and, if you like, speak the words aloud softly.

O Leader of Ancient Israel, send your Spirit to teach us your spirit of *Leadership* in guiding others in your way of peace. We make this prayer through Christ our Lord. Amen.

Closing Prayer

Psalm 20: Prayer for a Leader

May the LORD give you a favorable answer;
may the name of the God of Jacob set you up on high.
May he send you help from the sanctuary
and give you support from Zion.
May he bear in mind all your sacrifices,
and regard your holocausts as fat.
May he grant you what is in your mind
and bring to the full your whole design;
so that we may shout with joy for your victory
and set up our banners in the name of our God.
May the LORD fully answer all your petitions.
Now I know that the LORD has given victory to his anointed;
that from his holy heaven he has answered him
with mighty deeds — with salvation by his right hand.
Some rely on chariots and some on horses;

we, instead, invoke the name of the LORD our God.
They have bent their knees and fallen;
we, instead, have sprung to our feet and stand upright.
O LORD, save the king.
Answer us on the day we call.

A Song for Reflection and Meditation: "Answer When I Call"

Refrain: Turn an ear to me, O Lord;
              answer when I call. (Repeat)

Verses: Like an owl in the desert,
              a sparrow, alone and astray,
              I watch, I wait. (*Refrain*)

              Like the grass of the summer,
              like shadows, that wither and fade,
              O Lord, I wait. (*Refrain*)

              Give an ear to my pleading, and hear me,
              O God of my heart;
              I wait, I pray. (*Refrain*)

Questions for Spiritual Reflection

1. How do I define leadership? Managership? Does my understanding reflect both the positive and negative sides of leadership?

2. How do I live out the spiritual side of leadership? What do I do to nurture my own and others' "spiritual side"?

3. Am I aware of the opportunity as a leader that I have to bring about values like peace, dignity, and justice and not just a great bottom line?

Chapter 2

Empowerment

A Prayer to the Empowering Spirit

Holy Spirit of God, love of God, silent, secret, all
     preserving,
Breathing where you wish, expressing our longings.

You are wisdom, you are love, you are strength and
     fidelity.
I am in need of these.
I need them all, sincerely I want them,
I do believe sincerely I want them.

You do not fail. Will you fail me?
That I may never fail you, I cannot trust myself;
That I may never do wrong;
That I may be wise according to my place in life;
That I may love truly, not falsely;
That I may be faithful
to God, to people;
that I may have strength sufficient
for the task you give me and may
use it. Amen.

—Archbishop Goodier

THE SPIRITUAL LEADER EMPOWERS

Empowerment has become quite the organizational buzzword in the late 1980s and early '90s. Political administrations and corporate movers and shakers have used the term freely, and it has become burdened with some negative and cynical connotations. When used in a superficial way, it sounds like a positive concept, but used as a political "fuzzword" it becomes a euphemism or code expression for cutting people off, for shutting them out.

But taken at its best, unencumbered by any such baggage, the term empowerment means a humanistic exercise of power that frees people from problems of dominance or oppression. Empowering others allows them to freely express energy, talents, and gifts that will lead to a balance of power within any organization. The empowerment process involves motivating others, providing incentives for them to participate, and grappling with difficult issues. It is said that the best leaders are people who "let workers get the job done" and who give them the tools to do it. Organizational leaders who are able to empower others see better results and better spirit in the organization, and they are able to invite participation and inspire lasting loyalty. Perhaps that is why Thomas Moore writes that "In the soul, power doesn't work the same way as it does in the ego and will... we keep our power when we protect the power of others."

Brazilian writer and educator Paulo Freire has much to say about freeing others from various forms of oppression that occur in power conflicts. For the leader seeking a fresh way of looking at power and the bonds that go with it, he offers some unique perspectives in *Pedagogy of the Oppressed* (1970). Those who apply Freire's theory for educating the oppressed would demand that leaders and followers alike dialogue and think critically, affirm others in the process of growing and becoming, free others in making decisions, believe in one another's power to make, to create and recreate, and believe that one's work is to be fully human regardless of sex, age, race, or class. Freire writes that the communication that is central to the pedagogy of the oppressed is achieved when the leader, "educator, politician... understands the structural conditions in which the thought and language of the people are dialectically framed" (pp. 85-86).

Warren Bennis and Burt Nanus, in *Leaders: The Strategies of Taking Charge*, offer leaders a structure than can help them empower others in their own work place. The model suggests four critical dimensions for empowering others. We believe these are reflected in Christ's style of empowering leadership, illustrated in Table 2 below:

Table 2

BENNIS AND NANUS	CHRIST
1. *Significance*: The leader creates a vision that gives followers a feeling of being at the active center of the social order.	"For Jesus Christ, the Son of God... is God's 'Yes'; for it is he who is the 'Yes' to all of God's promises. This is the reason that through Jesus Christ our 'Amen' is said, to the glory of God" (2 Cor 1:19-20). Jesus created a spirit of excitement, acceptance and inclusion among his followers. Jesus included *everyone* — lepers, harlots, tax collectors.
2. *Competence*: The leader aims to develop followers and helps them to find meaning, a sense of mastery, new levels of performance, and commitment to organizational goals.	"Now once [Jesus] was in a certain place praying, and when he had finished one of his disciples said, 'Lord, teach us to pray'" (Lk 11:1). "All the people came to [Jesus], and after taking a seat he began to teach them" (Jn 8:2). "I tell you the truth: whoever listens to my words, and believes in the One who sent me, has eternal life..." (Jn 5:24). Jesus healed people and sent them on their way. Jesus forgave sinners and sent them out to new lives — to "go and sin no more."
3. *Experience of Community*: The leader instills feelings of common purpose or a sense of reliance on one another toward attaining a common cause.	"It is through Christ that both of us [Jews and Gentiles] have access in the one Spirit to the Father" (Eph 2:18). "The community of the faithful were of one heart and mind" (Ac 4:32). "He said to them, 'Go to the whole world and proclaim the good news to all creation'" (Mk 16:15).
4. *Enjoyment*: All leaders and followers are empowered and have fun in working toward a common vision and cause.	"The seventy-two returned joyfully..." (Lk 10:17). "Jesus said, 'Abide in my love... I've told you these things so my joy may be in you and your joy may be complete'" (Jn 15:10-11).

There are many biblical examples where Christ frees others. He seems to have a knack for making people feeling included, legitimate, and worthy. Jesus empowered small children when he put his arms around them, laid his hands on them, and gave them his blessing (Mk 10:13-16). John shows how he empowered the adulterous woman when he asked her, "'Has no one condemned you?' 'No one, Lord,' she replied. Then Jesus said, 'Neither do I condemn you. Go your way, and from now on sin no more'" (Jn 8:10-11).

Christ gave one of the most dramatic examples of his empowerment style by appointing Peter, a man who had denied him three times, as head of the Church:

> He asked his disciples, "But who do *you* say I am?" Simon Peter replied, "You are the Messiah, the Son of the Living God." In response Jesus said to him, "Blessed are you, Simon, son of John, for it wasn't flesh and blood that revealed this truth to you, but my Father in Heaven. And now I tell *you*, that you are Peter [Rock], and on this rock I will build my Church, and the gates of Hell will not prevail against it. I will give you the keys to the Kingdom of Heaven; whatever you bind on earth will be bound in Heaven and whatever you loose on earth will be loosed in Heaven." (Mt 16:15-19)

The key to empowering is taking on the spirit of Christ. Catholic theologian Avery Dulles once commented on the amazing variety of ways that people have come to be attracted to Jesus Christ. If one were to listen to all the men and women through the centuries who have found Jesus irresistible, all sorts of qualities and characteristics would emerge.

Naming something can be a great source of power. American Indians believe that to name a thing gives one power over it. Modern psychology teaches that to name a fear gives one control over it. Naming an experience is one way of discovering and enhancing one's potential for empowerment. Naming our own images of God can empower us and help us identify our own style of Christian leadership.

In *The Spirit Master*, theologian John Shea cites a number of ways of naming the Lord from which empowerment is derived. For many people Christ is Hope, Life, the Way, Word, Wisdom, Light, Judge, Teacher, Spouse, Victim, Lion, Sheep, Rock, or House. He is Priest, Prophet, Peace, or Precious Stone. For others, Christ is the Bridegroom of the Soul, the Mirror of the Eternal, Prince of Peace, Poet of the Spirit, Liberator, Mediator, or Messiah. Probably every single line in the Gospels has been, at some time or another, a source of empowerment for someone.

Shortly before her untimely death of cancer, Sister Thea Bowman, evangelist, author, and teacher, was asked what her images of God were and how they had changed over the years. Her response sheds light on the impact of naming experiences:

> I was reared in the traditional black community — in song and prayer and conversation and stories. My people graced me with multiple images of the living God.
>
> God is bread when you're hungry, water when you're thirsty, a harbor from the storm. God is a father to the fatherless, a mother to the motherless. God's my sister, my brother, my leader, my guide, my teacher, my comforter, my friend. God's the way-maker and burden-bearer, a heart-fixer and a mind-regulator. God's my doctor who never lost a patient, my lawyer who never lost a case, my chaplain who never lost a battle. God's my all in all, my everything.
>
> God's my rock, my sword, my shield, my lily of the valley, my pearl of great price. God's a God of peace and a God of war. Counselor, Emmanuel, Redeemer, Savior, Prince of Peace, Son of God, Mary's little baby, wonderful Word of God.
>
> These images come from Scripture and from the meditations of Christians. Some people see them as contradictory, but Christians see them as inadequate — all of them. But all these images are available to me. I meditate on each one of these images on a particular day at a particular time. Each one corresponds to a particular need. All these images help me as I call upon God's name. (*US Catholic*, April 1990, p. 22)

Sister Thea Bowman clearly demonstrates in this interview how she was personally empowered by integrating prayer into her experiences as a black woman who was converted from the Baptist tradition. She symbolizes her empowering experiences and names them in a variety of powerful images. The contemplative mode is evident in all of this.

Empowerment requires apprenticeship to Christ. Perhaps this is a difficult point for leaders who by virtue of their position are considered masters and not apprentices. But leaders who put themselves at the service — the apprenticeship — of Christ's example, will find the answers to questions like: What is it about Jesus Christ that impels so many to turn to him, to give themselves over to become his followers? What is it that engages leaders to be Gospel men and women? What empowers leaders to give themselves to his word and work?

In *The Spirit Master,* John Shea talks about how the spirit of the Master gets shared, gets passed around through a sort of osmosis. He points out that what happens is like what happened to the followers of Jesus who walked, talked, ate, and worked with him. Slowly they assimilated Christ's spirit and were thereby empowered. They took on the same style of leadership, the same way of thinking, the same way of preaching the good news, and even the same way of reacting to events and problems.

Empowerment, as practiced by Christ, is gained through prayer. Christ empowered himself by turning within. He often withdrew to the desert to pray, to recharge, to revitalize himself. Leaders must also be pray-ers and must turn within. There is a popular phrase, "To change one's outside, one must change what's inside." Through prayer and turning within, leaders can gain confidence that God is present in our struggle to find and give peace and joy. By turning within and rooting relations with God, we become a people with insight, vision, and courage.

Empowering others rests on taking on Christ's heart and mind and also taking on his leadership style. This is quite obvious in the following exchange between Jesus and Peter:

> After they'd eaten breakfast Jesus said to Simon Peter, "Simon son of John, do you love me more than they do?" He said to him, "Yes Lord, you know that I love you!" He said to him, "Feed my lambs!" Again he said to him a second time, "Simon, son of John, do you love me?" Peter said to him, "Yes, Lord, you know that I love you!" He said to him, "Tend my sheep!" Jesus said to him a third time, "Simon, son of John, do you love me?" Peter was distressed because he asked a third time, "Do you love me?" and he said to him, "Lord, you know everything; you know that I love you!" Jesus said to him, "Feed my sheep!" (Jn 21:15-18)

In following Christ's loving and compassionate ways, any leader can empower the suffering, the poor, the blind, the lame, and the lepers. The strength of this level of empowerment is gained by more deeply identifying with Christ's ways, and this can come best through prayer, just as he prayed.

Spiritual Reflection

Feeling powerless? Unsure how to give power to others? The following prayer is suggested for empowerment and for the ability to empower. Feel free to pray it anytime, anywhere. Take a moment, wherever you are — at your desk, in a meeting, in your car, and quietly, gently pray:

> *Empowering God*, teach us your spirit of *empowerment* that we may serve you faithfully. We ask this through Christ our Lord. Amen.

Perhaps you'd like to use the following prayer in a group setting, along with the closing psalm and song for empowerment.

Leader: Lord, you empower us — the human beings of this world — with the gifts of your Holy Spirit.

All: Open our hearts to your Spirit, so that we will use our humanity to make Christ present and active in our lives.

Guide us toward making our world a better place by realizing our human potential and helping to develop that
potential in others. Grant us a "daybreak" in which we
can illuminate the world with our Spirit. Kindle in us the
fire of your Spirit, against all odds and forever, in our
quest for you. Amen.

Closing Prayer

Psalm 8: A Psalm of Reflection on the Empowering and
        Powerful God

O LORD our God, how majestic is your name over all the earth!
Your praise resounds above the heavens.
On account of your opponents,
you have laid the foundations of a strong defense
on the speech of babes and infants,
to silence both enemy and antagonist.
When I contemplate your heavens, the work of your own fingers,
the moon and the stars, which you have fixed in place,
who are we that you should take thought of us —
that you should care for us?
Still, you have made us little less than the gods
and crowned us with glory and splendor.
You have given us dominion over the works of your hands;
all things have you set under our feet:
all of the sheep and oxen,
but also untamed beasts,
birds of the air, and the fish of the sea
  — whatever moves along the pathways of the seas.
O LORD our God,
how majestic is your name over all the earth!

Song of Empowerment

Refrain: *Till the end of my days, O Lord, I will bless your name.*
       Sing your praise, give you thanks, all my days.

You have made me little less than a god,
And have lavished my heart with your love.
With dignity and honor you've clothed me,
Given me rule over all.
You have blessed me with good things and plenty
and surrounded my table with friends.
Their love and their laughter enrich me;
together we sing your praise.
Your sun and your moon give me light
And your stars show the way through the night.
Your love and your laughter enrich me.
I will sing your praise.

Questions for Reflection

1. Can I name practical ways in which I empower others?

2. Do I create situations that include everyone? That allow them to share a common purpose?

3. How willing am I to share authority and a common purpose?

4. What are my images of God as the one who empowers? How does God empower me/us?

5. If I asked myself honestly if people enjoy working with me, what would the answer be? (If "no," is there a way to bring joy to what we do?)

Chapter 3

Attitude

PRAYER TO THE HOLY SPIRIT

O Holy Spirit, give me stillness of soul in you.
Calm the turmoil with the gentleness of your peace.
Quiet the anxiety within with a deep trust in you.
Heal the wounds of sin with the joy of your forgiveness.
Confirm the hope with the knowledge of your strength.
Give fullness to the love within with an outpouring of your
     love.
O Holy Spirit, be to me a source of light, strength, and
     courage so that I may hear your call ever more
     clearly and follow it more generously. Amen.

THE SPIRITUAL LEADER HAS A GREAT ATTITUDE

Our disposition plays a big part in the way we go about managing and leading. In *The Phenomenology of Feeling*, Stephen Strasser explores the phenomena of the heart: dispositions, intentional feelings, emotions, and passions. According to Strasser, disposition is the way in which you and I are disposed to the world. Disposition is an "a priori essential feature of being human — of being in the world" (p. 184). Disposition is what we bring into our ordinary life experience, day after day.

Strasser thinks that the feelings and actions we direct toward the world emerge from our dispositions and shape our experiences. These experiences in turn affect our disposition and ultimately our attitude. Strasser writes:

> All that pushes toward us in our becoming aware of the world and in our intimacy with the world, can move us and resonate in our innermost center.
>
> Stirrings, shaming, exalting events, successes, defeat, all have their dispositional reverberations. Ultimately everything lived through and experienced condenses itself into a "being-in-a-mood." (p. 185)

It is largely disposition that will shape the way we project our attitude toward leadership.

The spiritual model of leadership moves us toward adopting attitudes that lift spirits, arouse cooperation, or rise above problems. Lao Tzu summarized this predisposition when he said around 565 B.C.:

> A leader is best
> When people barely know he exists
> Not so good
> When people obey and acclaim him.
> Worse when they despise him.
>
> But of a good leader

Who talks little
When his work
His aim fulfilled,
They will say
"We did it ourselves."

If leaders have unpretentious and sincere attitudes, they inspire others to invest energy toward achieving organizational goals. Attitudes that lift others are crucial to putting the shared vision and mission into action.

This does not mean that a leader has to be a Pollyanna-like character who cannot acknowledge feelings of depression, dark moods or negative emotions. Thomas Moore in *Care of the Soul* argues that dark attitudes are sometimes essential in order to put persons in touch with themselves. He says that humans need to find a way to live with their disturbing feelings such as jealousy and envy, and that "anything so difficult to accept must have a special kind of shadow in it, a germ of creativity shrouded in a veil of repulsion... As we have so often found, in matters of the soul the most unworthy pieces turn out to be the most creative." Moore says that although attitudes or emotions like these can be corrosive to the soul, they can also be "poisons that heal" which eventually peacefully coexist within a soul. So, too, it is with depression. "Some feelings and thoughts seem to emerge only in a dark mood," he writes. "Suppress the mood, and you will suppress those ideas and reflections" (p. 137). If leaders "deny or cover up anything that is at home in the soul, then we cannot be fully present to others. Hiding the dark places results in a loss of soul; speaking for them and from them offers a way toward genuine community and intimacy" (p. 148).

So it is with leaders. The point is not to have consistently positive attitudes, especially falsely positive attitudes, but to have well-examined attitudes that give hope and power rather than oppression or fear to others.

In *The Knowledge Executive: Leadership in an Information Society*, Harlan Cleveland, a former diplomat, university president,

and dean of the University of Minnesota's Hubert H. Humphrey
Institute of Public Affairs, discusses four indispensable attitudes
for leadership in any organization. Table 3 below contrasts these
attitudes with those that Jesus taught.

Table 3

CLEVELAND	JESUS
Cleveland says that leaders hold:	Jesus said:
Notion that crises are normal, tension can be promising, and complexity is fun.	Anyone who loves his life for my sake, and for the Gospel will save it (Mk 8:35). Even the sparrows have God to take care of them. Why should you have any less? Let tomorrow take care of itself.
Realization that paranoia and self-pity are reserved for people who don't want to be executives.	Love your enemies and pray for those who persecute you (Mt 5:44).
The conviction that there must be some more upbeat outcome that would result from adding together the available expert advice.	How happy are the poor in spirit... those who mourn... those who hunger and thirst... are persecuted... theirs is the kingdom of heaven (Mt 5:3-10).
A sense of personal responsibility for the situation as a whole.	There are people with a noble and generous heart who have heard the word and take it to themselves and yield a harvest through their perseverance (Lk 8:15).

In his prayer *"Praütés,"* Peter G. Van Breemen captures in a single
Greek word the essential attitude toward life that characterized Jesus
in the Gospel. *"Praütés"* serves as a summary of the eight beatitudes and nine qualities of the Holy Spirit that profile the image of
a Christian. How happy are Christian leaders who are poor in spirit
and gentle, who mourn, hunger and thirst for what is right, are
merciful, pure in heart, peacemakers, and persecuted in the cause
of right (Mt 5:1-10). The Spirit brings to these leaders love, joy,
peace, patience, kindness, goodness, trustfulness, gentleness, and
self-control (Gal 5:22).

Van Breemen contends that the best translation of "*Praütés*" is a person who radiates a still heart. Christian leaders can find peace in assuming Christ's attitude if they internalize Matthew 11:29: "Learn from me, for I am gentle and humble in heart, and *you will find rest for your souls.*"

Christ's greatness in attitude was in obedience to what he discerned his Father wanted. In prayer, preaching in the synagogues, and in casting out devils, Christ responded to his Father's will. In our leadership capacities we need to be attentive to the voice of God not in isolation from society or apart from any political situation or social stratum: privileged, middle class, or penniless. In confronting whatever life brings to us, life or death, joy or sorrow, we need to assume the Christlike spirituality rooted in an attitude that acknowledges, "I can do nothing on my own; ... I seek, not my own will, but the will of the One who sent me" (Jn 5:30).

Any leader who asks as Philip did in John 14:8, "Lord, show us the Father and we'll be satisfied," needs to listen and to pray over the profound expression of Christ's obedience to God in response to Philip's request:

> Don't you believe that I am in the Father
> and the Father is in me?
> The words I speak to you I do not speak on my own,
> But the Father, Who abides in me, is doing His works.
> Believe me when I say that I am in the Father
> and the Father is in me;
> But if you don't,
> believe because of the works themselves.
> Amen, Amen, I say to you,
> Whoever believes in me,
> the works I do, he too, will do,
> And he'll do greater works than these,
> because I am going to the Father!
> And whatever you ask for in my name, I'll do,
> so the Father may be glorified in the Son. (Jn 14:10-13)

The prayerful leader in search of God's will sets the climate for adopting attitudes that lead to new levels of morality, morale, peace and joy among persons within any organization.

Paul's letter to the Philippians has a message for leaders who desire to assume Christ's attitude. He urges: "Do nothing out of selfishness or a desire to boast; instead, in a spirit of humility toward one another, regard others as better than yourselves. Each of you should look out for the rights of others, rather than your own. Have the same attitude among you that Christ Jesus had:

> Who, though he was in the form of God
> did not consider equality with God
> something to hold on to.
> Instead, he emptied himself and took on
> the form of a slave,
> born in human likeness,
> and to all appearances a man.
> He humbled himself and became obedient,
> even unto death, death on a cross.
> For this reason God exalted him
> and gave him a name above every other name,
> So that at the name of Jesus every knee shall bend,
> in the heavens, on earth, and below the earth,
>
> And every tongue will proclaim to the glory of God the Father,
> that Jesus Christ is Lord. (Ph 2:3-11)

Spiritual Reflection

In some circles, people jokingly call "happy hour" an attitude adjustment. Frustrated by work stress, co-worker conflict, problems at home, we all sometimes need an attitude adjustment. A moment of reflective and inward prayer offers an attitude adjustment that is far more effective than the short-term effects of any cocktail hour.

Take a moment in a quiet place to pray and reflect upon the following:

There are different kinds of spiritual gifts but the same Spirit;
there are different forms of service but the same Lord; there
are different workings but the same God who produces them
all in everyone. To each individual the manifestation of the
Spirit is given for some benefit. To one is given through the
Spirit the expression of wisdom; to another the expression of
knowledge according to the same Spirit; to another faith by
the same Spirit; to another gifts of healing by the one Spirit;
to another mighty deeds; to another discernment of spirits; to
another varieties of tongues. But one and the same Spirit produces all of these, distributing them individually to each person as he wishes. (1 Cor 12:4-11)

A Closing Prayer for Attitude Adjustment

Almighty God, increase your Spirit within us to lift our own
and others' *attitudes* in following Christ. We make this prayer
through Christ our Lord. Amen.

Psalm 72: The Reign of the Messiah

God, teach the king [read *the leader*] your ways of judging
and the king's son your justice
that he may judge your people justly,
and your poor, rightfully.
May the mountains as well as the hills
bring forth peace to the people through justice.
May he be a judge for the poor of the people,
and a defender for the children of the needy.
May he, instead, crush the oppressor.
People will revere you as long as the sun lasts
and as long as the moon exists — throughout all generations.
May he be like rain that flows down on the mown grass,
like showers moistening the earth.
In his time, may the righteous man blossom
as well as great peace, until the moon is no more.
He will have dominion from sea to sea,

and from the River up to the utmost bounds of the world.
Desert inhabitants shall bend their knee before him,
and his enemies shall lick the dust.
Kings from Tarshish and the isles
shall bring gifts;
kings from Sheba and Seba shall offer presents.
All kings, moreover, shall pay him homage;
all the nations shall be his servants.
For he will deliver the poor man who cries for help,
as well as the humble man who is helpless.
He will sympathize with the weak and the poor
and defend the lives of the needy:
he will deliver their lives from oppression and violence;
yes, in his eyes their blood will be precious indeed.
So long may he live and be given the gold of Sheba;
may prayers be offered for him unceasingly;
may they bless him all the time.
May there be plenty of corn in the land
to the summit of the mountains,
with its fruit waving like Lebanon.
May people flourish in the cities like fresh grass on the earth.
May his renown be everlasting;
as long as the sun lasts, may his renown spread;
and may every nation be blessed in him,
and pronounce him blest.
Blessed be the LORD God, the God of Israel,
who alone works wonders,
and blessed be his glorious name forever.
And may the earth at large be filled with his glory.
Amen and Amen.

A Song that Uplifts Attitudes

Refrain: Lift up your hearts to the Lord!
                In praise of God's mercy
                Sing out your joy to the Lord.
                God's love is enduring.

Verses: Shout with joy to the Lord, all the earth!

Praise the glory of God's name!
Say to God, "How wondrous your works!
How glorious Your name!" (*Refrain*)

Let the earth worship, singing Your praise.
Praise the glory of Your name!
Come and see the deeds of the Lord;
come worship God's name! (*Refrain*)

At God's touch, the dry land did appear;
Paths were opened in the sea;
let the earth rejoice in God's might,
the might of God's love. (*Refrain*)

Questions for Reflection

1. Does my disposition uplift others or cause problems? Do I bring out the best or worst in others?

2. Am I aware of the effect my attitude has on others? Am I approachable? Am I moody?

3. What of Christ's attitudes could I adopt for my own?

Chapter 4

Dialogue

A Prayer to the Spirit Who Listens and Speaks

Divine Spirit,

One with God the Creator and the Son,
Deign at this hour to come down on us without delay
And pour out your grace over our soul.

Let mouth, tongue, soul, thought, and strength
Make your praise resound.
Let our love be set aflame by the fire of your love
And its heat in turn enkindle love in our neighbors.

Grant this, most loving Creator,
And you, the only Son, equal to the Creator,
and, with the Spirit, the Paraclete,
reigning through the ages. Amen.

THE SPIRITUAL LEADER DIALOGUES

The spiritual side of leadership means mastering dialogue. To the Jewish philosopher Martin Buber genuine dialogue meant not only thinking, talking, and reasoning together, but also an all-out effort to establish mutual respect and understanding. Buber believed "people need to know each other," relating to one another not as object (I-It), but as subject (I-Thou). This kind of dialogue can overcome hatred, anger, and resentment. By meeting face to face with our perceived enemy, by speaking our mind, and by remaining what we are, we can affirm the "loving presence of each other." Dialogue is the very essence of communication between leader and followers and is inseparable from effective leadership.

Thomas Mitchell discusses dialogue in a remarkable essay, "I Can't Hear, But I Can Listen" (*The New York Times*, 1989). The essay tells of his experience in trying to cope with hearing loss after a bout with meningitis. Mitchell recounts a conversation he had with a total stranger who was easy to lip-read. The two talked for an hour about many things. At one point the stranger said to Mitchell: "I really enjoyed talking with you." Mitchell asked, "Why so?" The stranger said, "Because you are such a good listener." This response was quite complimentary for someone who had had impaired hearing for almost 20 years. The stranger explained: "Normal people hear a lot more than they listen. You on the other hand, can't hear a thing. You have to work to understand me. So at least in your mind you are really listening. Odd as it may seem, being deaf makes you listen better." This story illustrates that dialogue involves listening as much as it does talking.

Communications expert Bert Decker analyzes the process of communicating in his book, *You've Got to Be Believed to Be Heard*. Decker says that speakers must appeal to listeners' "first brain," the place where emotions are located. Successful leaders of tomorrow, he says, need to learn to speak to people's emotions, their hearts. He cites some popular communicators such as Katie Couric, Walter Cronkite, and General Norman Schwarzkopf, and finds one quality they all share: the ability to connect on the human level. Interestingly, Decker advances the idea that not only must the message be truthful, but people must perceive that the messenger is open and honest.

U.S. Attorney General Janet Reno recently gave an outstanding example of such direct, heartfelt communication. When federal agents of the Bureau of Alcohol, Tobacco, and Firearms raided the Branch Davidian compound in Waco, Texas and killed David Koresh and 85 of his followers, Reno stood tall literally and figuratively in taking full responsibility for the tragedy. She said, "The buck stops here. It was my decision. I approved the plans using the best judgment on what we knew... on what we know now, obviously it was wrong." In a hearing in the U.S. House of Representatives, Congressman Conyers (D-MI) exploded at Reno, calling the government actions "a profound disgrace to law enforcement." He implied that she was trying to "rationalize the deaths." With emotion, Reno responded, "I feel more strongly about the deaths than you will ever know." She did not run for cover. She stood her ground with her superiors, reporters, the public. What she has communicated during her period in office is admirable and inspirational.

The so-called quality revolution, which has been sweeping U.S. and international organizations, is based on the theories of W. Edwards Deming, who is sometimes called the "Father of the modern quality movement." Deming's philosophy of quality improvement is premised on the notion of dialogue — leader to follower, follower to leader, follower to peer, etc. With true communication, hierarchies, linear systems, and rational bureaucratic ways of doing things can be transformed into a collective buy-in where everyone has decision-making responsibility. Leaders who cannot communicate can find themselves in an "emperor-has-no-clothes situation," surrounded by people who are afraid to tell the truth, to say what they think. Unless leaders fully endorse dialogue and the free flow of communication, they can deceive themselves not only about the morale of those within their organization, but also about the quality of the service or products coming from the organization. Quality improvement efforts require rethinking even the most basic human resource and organizational assumptions. But some of the organizations that have been implementing quality improvement ideas are wildly enthusiastic about the results they are seeing and the important role dialogue plays in the process.

Keith Davis, in an article entitled "Management Communication and the Grapevine," analyzes the way that information travels within an organization — with or without help from management. He found that the organizational grapevine can be an asset or a liability, depending upon how executives perceive and influence it. The grapevine, he says, is part of the informal communication along with formal communication. It will not be a liability leading to innuendo and isolation if managers improve formal communication and follow three well-known communication principles:

1. Tell people about what will affect them (job interest).

2. Tell people what they want to know, rather than simply what you want them to know (job and social interest).

3. Tell people soon (timing).

In short, Davis advocates that leaders take the time to communicate, to dialogue, to be open, honest and forthright. As Decker would say: take the time to make a connection on the human level.

Poet and former CEO Jim Autry wrote a book entitled *Love and Profit*. In a poem entitled "Threads," he writes about that connection that leads to dialogue:

> Sometimes you just connect, like that,
> no big thing maybe
> but something beyond the usual business stuff.
> It comes and goes quickly
> so you have to pay attention...
>
> Listen.
> In every office
> you hear the threads
> of love and joy and fear and guilt
> the cries for celebration and reassurance

and somehow you know that connecting those threads
is what you are supposed to do
and business takes care of itself.

In his first encyclical, written before the conclusion of Vatican II,
Pope Paul VI identified four basic characteristics essential to any
real and fruitful dialogue: clarity, humility, trust, and prudence. This
was written at a time when there was confusion and mistrust about
the nature of dialogue within the Church, and Pope Paul highlighted
its importance in any relation: "Dialogue is the encounter between
people, mediated by the world, in order to name the world... It is
in speaking their word that people, by naming the world, transform
it... [Dialogue] cannot exist, however, in the absence of a profound
love for the world and for people."

Paulo Freire argued that love is at the heart of dialogue when
he said:

> Dialogue cannot exist, however, in the absence of profound
> love for the world and for men. The naming of the world,
> which is an act of creation and re-creation, is not possible if
> it is not infused with love. Love is at the same time the foun-
> dation of dialogue and dialogue itself. It is thus necessarily
> the task of responsible subjects and cannot exist in a relation
> of domination. Domination reveals the pathology of love:
> Sadism in the dominator and masochism in the dominated.
> Because love is an act of courage, not of fear, love is com-
> mitment to other men. No matter where the oppressed are
> found, the act of love is commitment to their cause — the
> cause of liberation. And this commitment, because it is lov-
> ing, is dialogical. (*Pedagogy of the Oppressed*, p. 78)

So how do committed and loving Christian leaders dialogue with
followers in spreading Christ's message? Thomas Clancy, in *The
Conversational Word of God*, calls for reviving the art of spiritual
conversation. Clancy says that in the Gospels one finds that rela-
tively few of Christ's words were preached or proclaimed. Instead,
Christ is portrayed in conversation. He spends a large part of his

time in dealing with small groups. Jesus has a number of one-on-one encounters with persons like Andrew, Peter, the Samaritan woman, the man born blind, and many others. And through these dialogues, these persons were drawn to a closer relation with the Lord. They became more attracted to him and in the process became more committed followers.

Interestingly, it is at the table, in breaking bread together, that a great deal of dialogue takes place. Eating is traditionally a social activity, a sharing of community — hence the word communion. Statesmen negotiate treaties over food; executives make deals over lunch. Families share their day and celebrate holidays together around the table. Foods function as sacred offerings, sacrifice, relief for the poor in soup kitchens, penance, and sometimes shameful displays of wealth. For the Jews food embodied God's wisdom, and eating it established a binding covenant. Divine services were made explicit through prayers at meals.

The meals Jesus shared with his friends were full of depth and meaning and ultimately led to the breaking of bread at the heart of liturgical life. Parker Palmer in an article entitled "Staying at the Table" relates the significance of breaking bread, of community, fellowship, and dialogue in the context of the final meal Jesus would share with his followers.

> When the hour came he sat down at table with the apostles. And he said to them, "With what longing I have longed to eat this Passover with you before I suffer; for I tell you that I will not eat it again until it is fulfilled in the Kingdom of God."
>
> Then he took a cup, blessed it, and said, "Take this and divide it among yourselves, for I tell you I will not drink the fruit of the vine until the Kingdom of God comes."
>
> Then he took bread, blessed it, broke it, and gave it to them, saying, "This is my body which will be given up for you; do this in my remembrance." Likewise he took the cup after they had eaten and said, "This cup is the new covenant in my blood which will be poured out for you."
>
> "But, behold, the hand of the one who will hand me over is

on the table with me, because the Son of Man is going as it has been decided. But woe to the man through whom he's handed over!" And they began to argue among themselves as to which of them it could be who intended to do this.

Now a dispute also arose among them as to which of them should be considered the greatest. But he said to them, "The kings of the Gentiles lord it over them, and those who exercise authority over them are called 'benefactors.' But not so with you! Instead, the greatest among you shall be like the youngest, and the ruler like the one who serves. For who is greater: the one reclining at table or the one who serves?" (Lk 22:14-27)

Parker Palmer comments on this scene's irony. Jesus has brought the group together on the eve of his trial, torture, and death, and what does the group do? They move into an argument about who is the greatest among them. And what does Jesus do? He just keeps breaking the bread and passing the cup. Jesus stays committed to them. He stays with them at the table despite their trivial arguments.

Staying at the table is a good way for real dialogue to take place. But real dialogue takes effort. Americans live in a narcissistic culture and are virtually trained to be self-involved. As Thomas Moore writes in *Care of the Soul*, "The trick is to find a way to that water of transformation where hard self-absorption turns into loving dialogue with the world." Collective-bargaining and mediation experts know that at times of intense negotiation between labor and management, both sides can run up against a "brick wall." Each side has its own story to tell and might hear the concerns of the other side, but truly is unable to listen. That is exactly when both sides respect the unwritten rule of collective bargaining: *we must stay at the table*. Perhaps it is sheer perseverance in such situations — staying at the table — that allows true communication to occur.

And it is the same for the spiritual leader in any situation where dialogue needs to take place. Staying at the table where the Eucharist is celebrated makes it possible for dialogue, community, and leadership to blossom. Leaders who follow Christ must try to stay at the table and to dialogue with people in their communities, churches, and families. Parker Palmer asks how it was that Jesus was able to stay at the table. What was Jesus' secret? The answer rests with the love he had for his Father and for us. At the liturgical table, leaders, as followers of Christ, must remember Christ's unfathomable love in his death and resurrection. They must be able to express their love of God by offering the bread and the cup that give life.

The fine art of dialogue requires listening, mutual sharing, and paying attention, especially to the call of God in one's life. Through dialogue and prayer a leader can get a better sense of the call to leadership. Through listening, sharing, and prayer, leaders and follows might just learn something new or unexpected, go somewhere unknown, or confront some different darkness.

In practice real dialogue with God requires listening to one another, to Christ, and to the world around us. This active listening of leaders means getting involved in other people's problems in their time of need. It means taking risks in sharing and acting out of love.

Listening to Christ praying in the Gospel, leaders and followers can encounter him in a powerful way not unlike that of the woman at the well or of the disciples sitting with Jesus at the Last Supper. But in prayerful contemplation there is something distinctive about the listening. Listening to Christ involves openness and risk. For to listen to Jesus invites dialogue, which ultimately involves following and serving Christ through one another.

Do men and women manage, lead, empower, and dialogue differently?

Current research shows that men and women tend to stereotype one another. Judy Rosener in "Ways Women Lead" (*Harvard Business Review*, November/December 1990) follows that thinking. She found that men and women are different after all. Successful women run things their way and not as men do.

Rosener is a professor at the University of California - Irvine, and in her study described a "woman's way of leading" as "transformational" patterns using interpersonal skills that are interactive, inclusive, and personal. This is different from the traditional male way of leading, which she called leading by "command and control."

Rosener points out that men and women exhibit different styles in different situations. We have all experienced women who demonstrate authoritarian, combative, and punitive behavior, as well as warm and interactive behavior. We have also experienced men who are warm and caring, as well as those under pressure to command and control.

Deborah Tannen, in her best seller, *You Just Don't Understand*, emphasized the differences between men and women. She said that women are comfortable in dealing with qualitative things, beauty, and bringing order out of chaos. Men like quantitative and easy-to-measure things and issues without ambiguity.

Most of the studies of gender differences in leadership and management involve men and women at the top of large companies. The few women at the top who have been studied tend to be like men at the top of large companies. In getting to the top, these women were found to be similar to their male counterparts in motivation, commitment, and charisma.

Leaders need to work toward a healthy balance in drawing on the gifts of both male and female inheritance and experience — we need both. At the least let us forget sex-typing. What is needed are intelligent, adaptable, practical, efficient and compassionate managers and leaders, because we are human. Let us affirm humanitarian values that characterize both men and women.

Jesus modelled control and command and interactive and personal power. The strength of his control and command can be viewed when he was tempted in the wilderness by the devil who showed him all the kingdoms of the world and their splendor, saying "All these things I'll give you, if you'll fall down and worship me." But Jesus said to him, "Begone, Satan! For it is written,

The Lord your God shall you worship,
and Him alone shall you adore." (Mt 4:9-10)

The Holy Spirit will look after us, if we do not fall into the temptation to amass power, prestige, and possessions.

Jesus modeled interactive and personal power in his many
dialogues. One of the most powerful exchanges was between Jesus
and the Samaritan woman at the well of Sychar (Jn 4:1-42). As the
woman draws water, Jesus asks her for a drink. The woman is surprised at his request and asks: "How is it that you, a Jew, ask me, a
Samaritan woman, for a drink?" Jesus transcended the hostility of
the Jews and, with respect and compassion for the woman, revealed
himself to her:

> If you knew the gift of God and who it is who's saying to you,
> "Give me a drink," you would have asked him and he would
> have given you living water.

The woman understands his bodily thirst for water, but does
not understand Jesus' offer of quenching the thirst of her soul with
"living water" which will transform her life. She says: "Lord, you
have no bucket and the well is deep, so where will you get this living water?" Jesus taught her theology and spirituality when he replied:

> Everyone who drinks this water will thirst again. But who-
> ever drinks the water I'll give him will never thirst; instead,
> the water I'll give him will become a spring of water welling
> up in him to eternal life.

The woman asked Jesus: "Lord, give me this water so I won't
become thirsty and won't have to come here again to draw water."
Without being judgmental, Jesus asked her to call her husband and
she honestly admitted to not having one. Jesus let her know he was
aware of the number of husbands she had had. Astounded by his
words, she said: "I see that you're a prophet."

Jesus opened her insights into the difference between places of worship — Jerusalem or the mountain Gerizim — and the call to worship in "spirit and truth" when he said:

> Believe me, woman, the hour is coming when you'll worship the Father neither on this mountain nor in Jerusalem. You worship what you don't know; we worship what we know, because salvation is from the Jews. But the hour is coming, and is now, when true worshippers will worship the Father in spirit and truth, for indeed the Father seeks such people to worship Him. God is spirit, and those who worship Him must worship in spirit in and truth.

The woman said to him, "I know that the Messiah is coming, who is called the Anointed; when he comes he'll tell us everything." Jesus revealed himself to her when he said: "I who am speaking to you am he."

His disciples returned and were surprised to find him speaking to a woman. In a condescending way they asked: "What do you want from her?" "Why are you speaking to her?" We get a hint of Jesus' profound experience with the woman in his answer to his disciples, who were urging him to eat something: "My food is to do the will of the One Who sent me, and to bring his work to completion." The revelation of himself to the woman at the well was the work of his Father that she would help to spread.

In the meantime, the woman had run into town, empowered with the new truths taught to her by Jesus, and without her water jar. Bodily thirst seemed to lose significance to her spiritual thirst to share what she had learned from the Lord. With enthusiasm she spread the Good News among the Samaritans, and many believed in Jesus on the strength of her testimony.

Jesus transcended gender differences in speaking to the woman at the well. The feminine and masculine values modeled by Jesus and the woman at the well were human values that resulted in interactive exchanges. Jesus used his power to teach the woman theological truths, stimulate her spirituality, and inspire her to proclaim the good news to her neighbors. She in turn used her personal power to question Jesus, to speak the truth, to learn from him, and to spread the Good News. The interaction between Jesus and the woman demonstrated mutual respect for the various dimensions of personal power and cultural diversity. His respect for the woman resulted in a healthy exchange between a man and a woman — a model of behavior to be emulated.

Jesus respected all persons from different cultures, not just the Samaritans.

> He travelled throughout the whole of Galilee, teaching in their synagogues, proclaiming the good news of the Kingdom, and healing every disease and illness among the people. News of him went out though all of Syria, and they brought him all who were sick with various diseases and were suffering torments — the demon-possessed, epileptics, paralytics — and he healed them. And large crowds followed him from Galilee and the Decapolis and Jerusalem and Judea and from beyond the Jordan. (Mt 4:23-25)

Jesus set an example for coping with the growing cultural diversity within organizations. We need to develop sensitivity for how different cultures use and define time, and for how they establish relations and communicate. Acceptance and respect for cultural diversity facilitates coping with change. No one should be made to feel disadvantaged. Management and leadership styles that strive to transcend race, gender, and age-group differences will lead to quality, high performance, and satisfaction.

Many not-for-profit organizations, following the Lord's example, have always provided services to the poor, minorities, immigrants, the elderly, displaced workers, the physically challenged. In general, however, we have to admit that in the multi-cultural and multi-ethnic population of the U.S., management and leadership is still dominantly white and male. Affirmative action policies and procedures have had only limited effect in piercing the glass ceiling in many places; still, they have been instrumental in moving toward more equality in the workplace. Sensitivity to diversity on the part of managers and leaders, where it is in evidence, has led to considerable cultural competence within organizations.

Economics is driving us to tolerate diversity — the labor pool is increasingly made up of women and people of color. Increasingly, women are facing a need to work. They want careers and not just jobs; they want full lives as mothers and as professionals. In organizations where diversity is valued there is no glass ceiling.

Companies are moving from an assimilation model where everyone is socialized to be similar to a model that values diversity — common ground is set by establishing common goals and the different ways of reaching the ends are valued. Criteria for measuring performance are inclusive rather than exclusive. This spirit leads to resolution of conflicts and misunderstandings. Leaders and managers can set an *esprit de corps* where people feel valued regardless of their differences by remembering that

> The Spirit is the life-giver,
> The flesh is profitless;
> The words I speak to you are Spirit and life. (Jn 6:63)

> A certain lawyer stood up to put Jesus to the test and said, "Teacher, what must I do to gain eternal life?" Jesus said to him, "What's written in the Torah? How do you read it?" In reply he said, "You shall love the Lord your God with your whole heart and with your whole soul and with your whole strength and with your whole understanding, and you shall love your neighbor as yourself." Then Jesus said to him, "You have answered correctly; do this and you shall live." (Lk 10:25-28)

Jesus interacted with the woman at the well, with other Samaritans, Galileans, the young lawyer, his disciples, and all he met. By his words and actions Jesus modelled the four aspects of transformational leadership that Rosener describes as characteristic of women: charismatic leadership, inspirational leadership, intellectual stimulation, and individualized consideration. Gospel men and women have a model in Christ Jesus for exercising transformational leadership.

In his farewell discourse, Jesus taught the ultimate way to transform lives when he said:

> I give you a new commandment: love one another;
> As I have loved you, you too should love one another.
> All will know by this that you're my disciples,
> If you have love for one another. (Jn 13:34-35)

Spiritual Reflection

The following is a brief prayer for meditation and psalm for reflection:

Divine Power, turn our hearts so that we will *dialogue* with our sisters and brothers. We ask this through Christ our Lord. Amen.

Psalm 34: In Praise of God's Justice

I will bless the LORD at all times;
his praise is constantly on my lips.
It is in the LORD that my soul shall boast.
The humble shall hear of it and rejoice.
Join me in celebrating the greatness of the LORD,
and let us extol his name together.
I sought the LORD and he answered me;
he delivered me from all my fears.
Those who gazed on him were enlightened
and their faces were not made to blush.
This afflicted man here cried and the LORD heard,
and saved him from all his troubles.
The angel of the LORD is encamped
round about those who fear him, and delivers them.
Taste and realize how good the LORD is.
Happy the person who takes refuge in him.
Fear the LORD, you his saints,
for those who fear him are in want of nothing.
Lion cubs have been in need and gone hungry;

but those who seek the LORD shall not be in want of any good
    thing.
Come, my sons and daughters, listen to me;
let me teach you the fear of the LORD.
Who is the person who longs for life,
who desires days and days
to enjoy happiness?
Restrain your tongue from evil,
and your lips from speaking lies.
Depart from evil and do good;
seek peace and follow after it.
The eyes of the LORD are turned to the righteous,
and his ears are tuned to their cry.
The countenance of the LORD confronts the evildoers,
to scratch out their memory from the earth.
The righteous cried out, and the LORD heard
and delivered them from all their troubles.
The LORD is close to shattered hearts,
and saves those whose spirits are overwhelmed.
Many are the afflictions of the just,
but the LORD delivers him from them all.
He watches over all his bones,
not one of them shall be broken.
Evil causes the wicked man's death;
and those who hate the righteous shall be held guilty.
The LORD ransoms his servant's soul;
none of those shall be held guilty who take refuge in him.

Questions for Reflection

1. I try to hear what others are saying, but do I really listen? Do I listen to the Spirit?

2. Do I let dialogue flow in more than one direction? Do I share my honest thoughts and feelings?

3. How do I promote dialogue in my organization? What "tables" do I set to enhance dialogue?

4. How do I affirm the loving presence of others?

Chapter 5

Emotional Wisdom

A Prayer to the Spirit of Emotional Wisdom

Come, Holy Spirit,
Shine from heaven
The beam of your inspiring light.
Come, protector of the poor,
Come, giver of effective gifts,
Come, illuminer of hearts.

Comforter most true,
Dear friend of the soul
And sweet consolation,
You are our rest in toil,
In turmoil our calm,
And solace in tears.

Most blessed light,
Infuse the deepest reaches of the heart
In all your faithful people!
Without your power
We are nothing,
Nothing is sure.
Wash clean what is unclean,
Water what is parched,
Heal what is wounded,
Soften what is rigid,
Direct what has gone astray.

Give to your faithful ones
Who place their trust in you
Your seven holy gifts;
Grant us the benefit of virtue,
A way of life ending in salvation;
Grant us joy everlasting. Amen.

THE SPIRITUAL LEADER IS EMOTIONALLY WISE

The spiritual side of leadership means expressing emotional wisdom. Bennis and Nanus found role models of emotional wisdom among the 90 CEOs, university presidents, and renowned artists they studied. These leaders exhibited many of the characteristics of a child: enthusiasm for people, spontaneity, imagination, and an unlimited capacity to learn new ways of acting. These childlike qualities were blended with five skills of emotional wisdom. These leaders:

1. Accepted people as they are;

2. Approached relations and problems in terms of the present rather than of the past;

3. Treated those close to them with the same courteous attention that was extended to strangers and acquaintances;

4. Trusted others, even if the risk seemed great;

5. Did not seek constant approval and recognition from others.

Max DePree, author of *Leadership is an Art*, finds similar qualities in good leaders. The ideal leader, he says, embodies:

- Humanity, gentleness, and caring as management precepts;
- An understanding of the diversity of people's gifts, talents, and skills;
- Participative management, which begins with a belief in people's potential;
- Roving leadership that demands that we enable one another, have a sense of interdependence;
- Vitality in work experience and meaning to life that comes from the condition of one's heart, the openness of one's attitudes, and the quality of one's competence and fidelity to one's experience;

51

- Intimacy with one's work that leads to competence;
- Managerial story-telling to keep one's history and historical context and values alive.

What is striking about the concept of emotional wisdom is the ages that are spanned in its attainment. The one who is wise possesses traits of a child as well as characteristics of someone who has lived a long life.

Christian leaders in any organizational setting can find some understanding of the practice of emotional wisdom by reflecting on Solomon's wisdom. (Sometimes it takes Solomon's wisdom to lead any organization!) As king, Solomon felt unskilled in leadership and asked God for a "discerning judgment" in governing the people entrusted to him.

> The Lord appeared in a dream to Solomon… [and] said, "Ask what you would like me to give you." Solomon replied, "Now Lord my God, you have made your servant king in succession to David my father. But I am a very young man, unskilled in leadership. Your servant finds himself in the midst of this people of yours that you have chosen, a people so many its number cannot be counted or reckoned. Give your servant a heart to understand how to discern between good and evil, for who could govern this people of yours that is so great?" It pleased the Lord that Solomon should have asked for this. "Since you have asked for this," the Lord said, "and not asked for long life for yourself or riches or the lives of your enemies, but have asked for a discerning judgment for yourself, here and now I do what you ask. I give you a heart wise and shrewd as none before you has had and none will have after you."
> (1 K 3:5-12)

Jesus' wisdom emerged early in his life. After losing Jesus for three days, his parents found their 12-year-old son "in the Temple, seated in the midst of the teachers, both listening to them and asking them questions; and all those listening to him were amazed at his intelligence and his replies" (Lk 2:46-47). During his hidden life at Nazareth it is noted also that Jesus "grew and became strong and was filled with wisdom, and the grace of God was on him" (Lk 2:40).

Christ's reputation for emotional wisdom extended throughout his public ministry: "'What sort of word is this? — He gives orders to the unclean spirits with authority and power, and they leave.' And news of him went out to every place in the surrounding region" (Lk 4:36-37). Even during his last days he influenced people with his teachings. "And all the people came early in the morning to listen to him in the Temple" (Lk 21:38). Although many were amazed at his wisdom, Christ looked like a fool to Herod and like a rebel to many of his enemies.

So, too, it is with corporate fools and prophets. Leaders who have visions are often criticized as unrealistic, as being "before their time." Organizational whistle-blowers, who may be answering to value and ethics systems above that of the "official party line," are not rewarded as heroes but are reviled and cast out as pariahs, seen, like Christ, as rebels and mavericks. Recently the CEO of Eastman Kodak was summarily fired by its board of trustees. The reason? The investors, eager for rapid increases in the value of their stock, were not happy with his management style. In short, they knew that massive layoffs would produce quick profits, but this CEO had wanted to turn around the company and produce profits on a more reasonable, long-term time line. He thought that this could be achieved without the ruined lives and despair that go with lost jobs. His leadership style, though emotionally wise and well thought out, was not acceptable in this time of quick money. And like Christ, he was sacrificed because of what he believed.

Paul's First Letter to the Corinthians addresses Christ as the Power and the Wisdom of God:

> For the message of the cross is foolishness to those who are
> on their way to destruction, but for those who are being saved
> — for us — it's the power of God. For it's written,

> "I'll destroy the wisdom of the wise,
> and the insights of the intelligent I'll reject."
>
> Where is the wise man? Where is the scribe? Where is the skilled debater of this age? Hasn't God turned the wisdom of this world to foolishness? For since, in God's wisdom, the world was unable to come to knowledge of God with its own wisdom, God chose through the foolishness of our proclamation to save those who believe.
>
> Jews ask for signs and Greeks look for wisdom, but we proclaim Christ crucified — a stumbling block for Jews and foolishness to Greeks, but for those who have been chosen, both Jew and Greek alike, Christ the power of God and the wisdom of God; for God's foolishness is wiser than human wisdom, and God's weakness is stronger than human strength. (1 Cor 1:18-25)

The spiritual leader teaches and empowers not with skillful words of human wisdom alone but with "convincing proof of the power of God's spirit" (1 Cor 2:4). The wisdom that Christian leaders speak is spiritual maturity.

> We preach God's wisdom, a wisdom secret and hidden, which God ordained before the ages for our glory. None of the rulers of this age understood this, for if they *had* they never would have crucified the Lord of glory. But, as it is written,
>
> What eye has not seen nor ear heard,
> what human heart has not conceived,
> is what God has prepared for those who love Him. (1 Cor 2:7-9)

Spiritual wisdom is speaking in words taught by the Spirit. It is explaining spiritual truths to those who have the Spirit, to those who have the mind of Christ. James explains the wisdom from above when he asks:

> Who among you is wise and intelligent? Let him show it by his good life, with a humility born of that wisdom. But if you harbor bitter jealousy or selfish ambition in your heart, don't

> boast and lie against the truth. This is not the wisdom that comes down from above — this is earthly, worldly, and demonic! For where there is jealousy and selfish ambition there is also disorder and every kind of bad deed. The wisdom from above is first of all pure, then peaceable, kind, reasonable, and full of good fruits, impartial and sincere. The harvest of righteousness is sown in peace by those who are peacemakers. (Jm 3:13-18)

Spiritually mature leaders must remember that "God has brought us into union with Christ Jesus, and God has made Christ to be our wisdom. By him we are put right with God; we become God's holy people and are set free" (1 Cor 1:30). Spiritually wise leaders are not held captive by the deceit of human wisdom, which comes from teachings handed down by and from the ruling spirits of the universe, and not from Christ (cf. Col 2:8). Full life comes from union with Christ (cf. Col 2:8-10).

Ben Carson, M.D., a pediatric neurosurgeon at the Johns Hopkins Hospital, exemplifies Christ's growth in maturity, wisdom, and grace. Five years ago Dr. Carson performed a delicate brain operation on a child who was close to death. When he finished he said: "We've done all that we can do. Now it's up to God."

Dr. Carson's comment was carried in newspaper and television reports from a Johns Hopkins Hospital press conference in Baltimore. Reporters seized the remark because words were uttered that are not usually voiced by today's physicians under the bright lights of the media.

The story is extraordinary because it rests on the growth of emotional wisdom within an acclaimed surgeon. Ben Carson was born and raised in inner-city Detroit. He was a very poor black youngster who developed a very violent temper, uncontrollable at times, even destructive. At age 14 his violent temper gave him the scare of his life when he attempted to stab a teenager in the abdomen. The intended victim's life was miraculously spared when the knife struck the fellow's large metal buckle and broke.

Carson was terrified by what he had done, because he realized he was emotionally completely out of control. So he locked himself in his room for three hours, and in his desperation he turned to God because he remembered that his mother had always prayed when she needed help in her times of need.

He prayed and he prayed, and he said, "God, it's up to you. You must take this temper away from me." And that very day he started to read from the book of Proverbs. Recently Dr. Carson remarked that he has read from that book every day since, because "It is just full of advice on how to live." After that his life changed, and from that day on he adopted God, his heavenly Father, as his earthly Father, since he had grown up without a father. He said, "I began to feel that God was somebody you could talk to, somebody who would answer prayers and give you wisdom, and that's a relationship that has grown."

If a leader lacks wisdom, he or she should pray to God for it as did Solomon, Ben Carson, and countless other leaders. God will give the needed wisdom because God is generous and gracious. When you pray, you "must ask in faith and without doubting, for whoever doubts is like a wave on the sea which is driven and tossed about by the wind. Such a person, who wavers and is undecided in everything he does, should not expect to receive anything from the Lord" (Jm 1:6-8).

Spiritual Reflection

Every day we see the results of actions by leaders — world leaders or organizational leaders — who are not emotionally wise. Perhaps they let themselves act out of emotions like fear, petulance, anger or revenge. It is difficult sometimes to discern what emotions are the wise ones in a given situation, but an emotionally wise leader can live with a stable emotional tone from which actions and decisions can be made. When in doubt, pray! Acknowledging the wonder of God is the first step toward true wisdom. In times of trouble or indecision, pray the following brief prayer for emotional wisdom. Take the time to praise the great works of the Lord with the psalm that follows.

A Prayer for Emotional Wisdom

Ever-loving God, bless us with the *emotional wisdom* that will lead us and others faithfully on our way to you. We make this prayer through Christ our Lord. Amen.

Psalm 111: The Great Works of God

Alleluia.
I will give thanks to the LORD with a whole heart
at the meeting both of the upright and of the congregation.
The accomplishments of the LORD are great,
an object of reflection for all who are fond of them.
His performance is all splendor and majesty,
and his righteousness stands forever.
He has made himself a memorial for his wonders.
The LORD is gracious and compassionate.
He gives nourishment to those who fear him,
he keeps his covenant in mind forever.
In giving to his people the possession of the nations
he has made known to them the power of his deeds.
The accomplishments of his hands are both truthful and right;
all his precepts are to be trusted,
unshakable for an eternity of eternities,
instituted according to truth and uprightness.
He sent deliverers to his people,
set up his covenant to last for ever.
His name is holy and awe-inspiring.
Fear of the LORD is the beginning of wisdom.
A good understanding have those who practice them.
Praise of him will last forever.

Questions for Reflection

1. What is the emotional tone from which I act and live? Do I consider it wise?

2. Do my actions offer "convincing proof of the power of God's spirit"? In other words, do my actions, not just my words, show that I have emotional wisdom?

Chapter 6

Renewal

For a Holy Heart

Lord, grant me a holy heart
that sees always what is fine and pure
and is not frightened at the sight of sin
but creates order wherever it goes.
Grant me a heart that knows nothing
of boredom, weeping and sighing.
Let me not be too concerned
with the bothersome thing I call "myself."
Lord, give me a sense of humor
and I will find happiness of life
and profit for others.

— St. Thomas More

Song to the Holy Spirit (Veni Sancte Spiritus)

Breathe here, now, and kindle me,
send me from your farthest distance,
surging light.
Welcome, poor folk's father;
welcome, chief cupbearer;
welcome, hunter of hearts.
Gentlest dryer of tears,
loving soul-indweller,
my friend, my shadow.
Restful moment
for drudgers and toilers
and breathing-spell for spastic kids are you.
Impossibly lovely light,
overflow the abyss
that you know so well, my heart.
You are God, without you
only night, untimely time,
violence and guilt.
You make me clean,
you soothe my wounds,
give water to my withered flower.
I stand stiff, read *No Admittance,*
am icebound, melt; embrace me;
I go astray, come seek me.
I tell you Yes, do No;
repay my doubt with friendship
seven times a thousand times.
Without you I am nothing.
Dear, I would go to you.
Then, I'll be laughing!
              Excerpted from *At Times I See*, freely translated.

THE SPIRITUAL SIDE OF LEADERSHIP IS RENEWAL

The spiritual aspect of leadership involves renewal. John Gardner, former Secretary of HEW (1965-68) and current Director of the Leadership Studies sponsored by INDEPENDENT SECTOR, states that renewing is one of leadership's most important tasks. Leaders need to be attentive to the times and stir themselves to action if they wish to break from or avoid the status quo. As shapers of what might be, leaders should be life-giving to persons and organizations, to enable them to grow and change with the changing times. Leaders need to find ways to awaken the potential within persons and organizations, to bring forth new levels of performance and life.

There is an old saying that "the only constant in life is change." Just as the seasons must continually change, so must people and organizations. Perhaps this is more true than ever before. Organizations in stasis become paralyzed and sick. And everyone is scrambling to keep pace with the ever-increasing rate of change brought on by science and technology, fiercely competitive economic conditions and changing societal values. Organizations are learning that to survive they need to change, evolve and respond not on a one-year or two-year basis, but on a monthly or weekly basis. Managers and leaders are expected to be change agents, whatever that means. And "changing corporate culture" is seen as a highly desirable activity. Authors make fortunes on "trend" books that predict coming changes. Perhaps now more than ever, change is an issue not just for organizations but for everyone alive. And change calls forth constant renewal. In fact, an organization's very survival may rest on *renewal*.

Organizations today face a dynamic environment that requires leaders to be continually renewing. Increased international competition, deregulation, threats from corporate raiders, mergers, growth in information technology, changing societal values, and tumultuous politics all have an impact on the expectations and preferences of people outside and within an organization. Today's leader is expected to renew the organization. And, as it evolves, this includes renewing the organization's goals, its mission, and perhaps its activities. But spiritually developed leaders must go deeper still to renew the hearts of those who work within the organizations; most important, they should remember to renew themselves.

Leaders, however, need to be discriminating in their renewal efforts. They cannot always rely on old visions and old objectives. Sometimes that is appropriate. Change should not be made for the sake of change alone. In a rapidly changing world, however, old objectives can become obsolete. A wise leader knows when and how to initiate change that will preserve the beliefs, values, and mission of persons and of the organization. "Hold onto the old as long as it is good. Embrace the new as soon as it is better."

Max DePree, in *Leadership is an Art*, states that constant renewal means being ready for the inevitable crises of corporate life. "Tribal storytelling" in organizational cultures is at the heart of renewal. "Storytellers" and "tribal elders" work at corporate renewal by preventing successful entrepreneurship and corporations from becoming institutions that foster bureaucracy. They preserve, revitalize, and nourish corporate values that eradicate bureaucracy and sustain people.

> The goal of renewal is to be a corporate entity that gives us space to reach our potential as individuals and, through that, as a corporation. Renewal comes through genuine service to others. It cannot come about through a process of mere perpetuation. Renewal is an outward orientation of service, rather than an inward orientation of maintenance. Renewal is the concern of everyone, but it is the special province of the tribal storyteller. (*Leadership is an Art*, p. 80)

In *Leadership Jazz*, DePree tells the touching story of his own personal renewal as a leader. He describes the birth of his granddaughter, Zoe, who was born prematurely.

> She weighed one pound, seven ounces, so small that my wedding ring could slide up her arm to her shoulder. The neonatologist who first examined her told us that she had a five to

ten percent chance of living three days. When Esther and I
scrubbed up for our first visit and saw Zoe in her isolette in
the neonatal intensive care unit, she had two IV's in her na-
vel, one in her foot, a monitor on each side of her chest, and a
respirator tube and a feeding tube in her mouth.

To complicate matters, Zoe's biological father had jumped
ship the month before Zoe was born. Realizing this, a wise
and caring nurse named Ruth gave me my instructions. "For
the next several months, at least, you're the surrogate father.
I want you to come to the hospital every day to visit Zoe, and
when you come, I would like you to rub her body and her legs
and arms with the tip of your finger. While you're caressing
her, you should tell her over and over how much you love her
because she has to be able to connect your voice to your
touch." Ruth was doing exactly the right thing on Zoe's behalf (and, of course, on my behalf as well), and without realizing it she was giving me one of the best possible descrip-
tions of the work of a leader. At the core of becoming a leader
is the need always to connect one's voice and one's touch.

Renewal in today's organizations often comes under the rubric of
organizational development or OD, a systems-oriented approach
to change. The term is actually used for a variety of change-ori-
ented activities aimed at enhancing abilities of organizational members to manage their culture in adapting to the external environment. Most OD interventions are directed at changing attitudes and
behaviors of organizational members through a variety of techniques including team building, sensitivity training, survey feed-
back, process consultation, and other types of group work.

But renewal efforts of leaders can go above and beyond OD
interventions because renew means "to make new spiritually." A
renewed spirit calls for a conversion of heart and mind. It means
being open to the Spirit within oneself and in others who hold different perspectives. It means opening to the Spirit in changing times.
It means surviving on the strength of the Spirit in a controversial
or political environment. It means empowering others to contrib-
ute to the success of organizational renewal.

Pope John XXIII was a great example of a leader in renewal. At age 76 he called the Catholic Church "to open its windows and let the fresh air in." His risk-taking behavior, imagination, and creativity all converged to make him the greatest leader for renewal in the Church during the 20th Century.

The renewal called for by Vatican II continues today with an emphasis on a faith that does justice. Religious and lay persons around the globe are involved in:

- confronting corporations, governments, and other institutions that restrict others in their human rights, religious freedom, or political expression;
- breaking down structures that discriminate against the poor, the aged, or racial or religious minorities;
- advancing public policies and social attitudes that protect the unborn, the unemployed, the handicapped, migrants, women, children;
- bringing the "Good News" to the poor, the unemployed, landless peasants, the aged, and minorities.

While visiting Northern Ireland, Father Daniel Berrigan heard a story about the famous round towers outside Dublin that illustrate the process of renewal. Apparently, in the sixth century and thereafter, when barbarians swept through the country, the monks built towers to protect themselves and some of the countryside people. They took only holy cups and the Bible with them to the towers. Periodically they would leave the tower in attempts to restore the countryside, to heal, and to start again. The dynamics of the story, the taking of the Bible and the cups, the restoring and the healing all symbolize the Eucharist.

In applying this story to the 20th Century, Berrigan asked: "What do we need absolutely in order to retain some version of humanity in an utterly savage time? The monks and people of the sixth century preserved a whole tradition in taking the holy cup and the Bible. Everything was not gone. They read the Scriptures and celebrated the Eucharist. The book of Christ was kept warm upon the altar and the memory of Christ green among his people" (*Pax Christi*, Fall 1989, p. 36).

Renewal in Christ is kept alive every day through the Eucharist — taking the holy cup, the healing power, the coming together at table. The preface of a proposed new Eucharistic Canon highlights God's ongoing creation and renewal:

> Blessed are you, strong and faithful God.
> All your works, the height and the depth,
> echo the silent music of your praise.
>
> In the beginning your Word summoned light:
> night withdrew, and creation dawned.
> As ages passed unseen
> waters gathered on the face of the earth and life appeared.
>
> When the times at last had ripened
> and the earth grown full in abundance,
> you created in your image man and woman,
> the crown of all creation.
>
> You gave us breath and speech,
> that all the living
> might find a voice to sing your praise.

As the Eucharistic Canon continues, God's nurturing and renewing the world through his Son and the Holy Spirit are acclaimed:

> All holy God,
> how wonderful the work of your hands!
> You restored the beauty of your image
> when sin had scarred the world.
>
> As a mother tenderly gathers her children,
> you embraced a people as your own
> and filled them with longing
> for a peace that would last
> and for a justice that would never fail.
>
> Through countless generations

your people hungered for the bread of freedom.
From them you raised up Jesus, the living bread,
in whom ancient hungers were satisfied.
He healed the sick
though he himself would suffer;
he offered life to sinners,
though death would hunt him down.
But with a love stronger than death,
he opened wide his arms
and surrendered his spirit.

The conclusion of the Canon states that the ultimate expression of self-renewal in God's love rests in prayer:

Father, we commemorate Jesus, your Son,
as we offer you this sacrifice.
Death could not bind him,
for your raised him up in the Spirit of holiness
and exalted him as Lord of creation.
May his coming in glory find us ever-watchful in prayer,
strong in love,
and faithful to the breaking of the bread.

Jesus brought renewal to the world. But recognizing that one's heart must be renewed before one can do any good in the world, Jesus took time regularly to withdraw in solitude and to pray. He withdrew to the desert to renew and "recharge" through inward reflection and prayer. It is important for today's leader to recognize that self-renewal is essential before outward renewal can happen. Through prayer, leaders turn inward to gather strength, replenish, de-stress, discern God's will, and better come to know their own motivations, emotions and values.

Through prayer people's hearts are renewed. Hearts of stone can be transformed into hearts that are compassionate, merciful, loving, and good. Through our renewed hearts we are ready to feed the hungry, to give drink to the thirsty, to clothe the naked, to visit the sick. Through renewed hearts leaders become ready to admonish the sinner, to instruct the ignorant, to forgive all injuries, to pray for the living and the dead.

A Prayer for Renewal

Feeling the need to recharge, replenish and renew? Just as the potter shapes the clay, leaders need to be open to reshaping their own thoughts, visions and behavior, and to be instrumental in shaping others. Prayer at time of renewal is essential in discerning God's will and reshaping of one's heart.

Take a moment to quietly pray the following prayer for renewal and the psalm that follows for a clean heart. If you like, use the song "Create in Me a Clean Heart" for meditation.

Renew us, O Lord, let us grow in your love and through your love all the days of our life. We ask this through Christ our Lord. Amen.

Psalm 51: *Miserere*

Be gracious to me, O God, as befits your loving kindness.
In the great tenderness of your love, wipe out my transgressions.
Wash me thoroughly from my guilt
and from my sin cleanse me;
for I realize my transgressions
and my sins are always before me.
It is against you, against you alone, that I have sinned,
and what is evil in your sight — this I have done;
so you are right when you speak up,
above suspicion when you pass sentence.
Clearly, I was born in guilt;
indeed, my mother conceived me in sin.
Clearly, you love truth in the depths of one's soul;
teach me wisdom, then, in my innermost being.
Purify me with hyssop, and I shall be clean;
wash me, and I shall become whiter than snow.
Let me hear joy and gladness.
Let the bones that you have crushed rejoice.
Hide your face from my sins

and wipe out all my guilt.
Create a clean heart for me, O God.
and renew within me an upright spirit.
Do not cast me out from your presence,
and do not hold your Holy Spirit back from me.
Restore me to the joy of your salvation,
and let a spirit of willingness uphold me.
I will teach transgressors your ways,
so sinners will come back to you.
God, my saving God,
deliver me from bloodshed,
and my tongue will glorify your righteousness with joy.
Lord, open my lips,
and my mouth will declare your praise,
for you take no pleasure in a sacrifice, should I offer it;
a holocaust you do not graciously receive.
God's sacrifices are a contrite spirit:
God, you cannot make little of a contrite, shattered heart.
(In your good will be benevolent to Zion:
repair the walls of Jerusalem.)
Then will you take pleasure in sacrifices of righteousness,
whether holocausts or whole offerings.
Then will they offer young bulls on your altar.

A Song for Renewal: "Create in Me"

Create in me, a clean heart, O God.
Create in me, a clean heart, O God.
Create in me, a clean heart,
and a new spirit within me.
Cast me not out of your presence Lord, and
deprive me not of your holy spirit.

Create in me, a clean heart, O God.

Questions for Spiritual Reflection

1. As a leader, how can I be an instrument of renewal for those I lead?

2. Do I take time to renew myself on a personal basis?

3. Do I use prayer as a means to renew my own heart?

Chapter 7

Shaping a Vision

Indian Prayer

O Great Spirit, whose voice I hear in the winds
     And whose breath gives life to all the world, hear me.
I am small and weak, I need your strength and wisdom.
     Let me walk in beauty, and make my eyes ever behold
     The red and purple sunset.
Make my hands respect the things you have made
     And my ears sharp to hear your voice.
Make me wise so that I may understand the things
     You have taught my people.
Let me learn the lessons you have hidden in every leaf and rock.
     I seek strength, not to be greater than my brother or sister,
     but to fight my greatest enemy — myself.
Make me always ready to come to you with clean hands and
     straight eyes.
     So when life fades, as the fading sunset,
     my spirit may come to you without shame.

THE SPIRITUAL LEADER SHAPES A VISION

In the last chapter we discussed renewal as integral to the spiritual side of leading. When a leader realizes the need for major renewal of the organization, the next step is to find ways to inspire people to shape a vision for a better future. The leader is mindful of the proverb: "Without a vision, the people perish" (Pr 29:18).

The spiritual leader shapes an achievable, clear, and compelling vision. This vision conveys where the organization is going, where the employees are heading, and why they should be proud of the direction. Its core is the organization's mission.

An effective vision is "right for the times, right for the organization, and right for the people who are working in it." The genius of a leader in articulating a vision is to make it simple enough to evoke commitment and credible enough to be accepted as realistic and attainable.

In the popular leadership book *In Search of Excellence*, Peters and Waterman describe the vision of several leaders of some of America's most successful companies. The success of Disney World and of Johnson & Johnson is based on a vision of corporate values. The success of McDonald's and of North American Tool and Die is based on a vision of concern for people.

Harold Leavitt, an expert on leadership, states that "Vision, values, and determination add soul to the organization. Without them, organizations react but do not create; they forecast but do not imagine; they analyze but do not question; they act but do not strive. While pathfinding vision, values, and determination are not enough, we can't go very far without them" (*Corporate Pathfinders*, pp. 222-23).

In *A Passion for Excellence*, Peters and Austin stress that successful leaders root their visions within the realities of the times and within the grasp of the people. Leaders with vision love what they do and care passionately in sharing a vision. These soaring ideals and values are gifts that inspirit — that set fire to the hearts of others in shaping and living the realities of a vision.

Bennis and Nanus, in their five-year study of 90 effective leaders (60 corporate leaders and 30 leaders of public-sector organizations) found that all had a vision of a desirable and possible future for their organizations. Sometimes it was a vague dream, sometimes a concrete mission statement. These leaders paid attention to what was going on, determined what events would be good for the future of the organization, set new direction, and won the commitment of everyone in their organizations to the new vision. It is important to note, too, that these leaders probably had a talent for dialogue and empowerment — by their including everyone in the vision, people feel they can be part of the vision. They invest themselves in it.

Two researchers, Tichy and Devanna, found in their interview studies of leaders that successful visions in large mature organizations are rarely the product of a single person. To be a source of self-esteem and common purpose for members, a vision needs to evolve and to be the product of a participative process. People must embrace the vision for it to be successful. Even in institutions characterized by centralization or crisis, where members expect leaders to propose solutions, participation is essential to guard against regression to old ways.

Whether people will commit to or invest themselves in a vision depends upon their trust — or lack of it — in leaders. This trust, in turn, depends upon how they perceive the leaders' expertise as well as how consistent the leaders' actions are with their statements. ("Do as we say and not as we do" management is far too often the example set by many leaders.) If people see inconsistency and do not trust their leaders, the vision becomes blurred and unappealing.

If a leader is unable to maintain a clear vision, it may be due to changing times, rapid technological change, increased diversification caused by mergers and acquisitions, or overemphasis on the "bottom-line" mentality among executives. Jimmy Carter was said to be lacking in creativity to shape a vision, but history and time have shown that he has been able to focus on problems in practical ways, for example, by going out and building homes for the poor through *Habitat for Humanity*. On the other hand, Ronald Reagan and Jesse Jackson, through their "gift of tongue," inspired visions and galvanized others to follow them, yet some people believe that their oratorical skills and image-creating ability are not followed through by practical or even symbolic actions that do anything to support the values they espouse. They lacked the practical "doing skills" that meet needs and produce results. Mitch Snyder, too, had a vision to help the homeless, and a number of people followed him. If Carter lacked the ability to create images that appealed to people, Reagan, Jackson, and Snyder, while talented at evoking symbols, lacked operational and institutional leadership in effecting systemic organizational change.

Ideally, a leader will have the ability to create a clear vision that people will follow, and will be able to find practical ways to put this vision into operation. Edgar H. Schein, an authority on organizational culture, says that in shaping a vision, it is not enough to set goals and sell symbols. The goals, symbols, and assumptions underlying the vision must fit with other deep cultural assumptions. Schein provides an anecdote of a leader who failed to use deeper visions before he sold his ideas.

During Atari's history, Warner Communications (the parent company) hired a former marketing executive from the food industry as president. This executive assumed that the key to success was high motivation and high rewards based on individual performance. He created and implemented an incentive system, which led to motivating individual engineers with large monetary rewards. In time some of the best engineers left because the new executive did not shape, articulate, and enforce a vision of an incentive system in keeping with the values of the engineers, who were used to working as a team. These workers were happy as group members and responded best to group incentive. The new president did not sense the internal and external cultural factors. That president of Atari lost his job, and the company was left with a challenge to restore its waning vision without his leadership.

In contrast, D.J. DePree, founder of Herman Miller, Inc., of Zeeland, Michigan, has had long-term success with the company vision shaped in 1932. The DePrees are known as "a strongly religious family" supportive of the "old virtues" that characterize corporate culture. A Christian philosophy underlies quality product, innovation, customer service, and employee involvement, and accounts for the company's success. Employees are moved to higher levels of consciousness as they design, make, and market innovative furniture. "Annual meetings begin with a prayer, alcohol is neither served at company functions nor allowed on expense accounts. Top executives refer to their stewardship of product, and their covenant with their employees" (A.M. Morrison, *Fortune*, June 15, 1981, p. 164).

In seeking a vision, Christian leaders can follow the example of the early Christians who relied on prayer and fasting to see more clearly the vision of Christ. These activities were viewed as essential to becoming more Christlike and free of the evil spirit.

The previous chapter talked about the importance of renewal, and about how Jesus took time to renew his own heart through solitude, fasting and prayer. The Christian leader may find this an ideal way to seek a vision, and should be ready to fast and pray as Christ did. Visioning that springs from seeing with Christ's eyes, hearing with his ears, imitating his actions, putting on his heart and mind, will lead to what is good.

> To act justly,
> to love steadfastly, and
> to walk humbly with God. (Micah 6:8)

In seeking a sublimated vision, Christian leaders can learn something from North American Indians. Since silence and prayer are part of the traditional way of living for Native Americans, their contemplative life is reflected in the way that they praise the Creator and revere the earth.

The vision of the great Indian Chief Black Elk near his life's end is similar to Christ's own vision. Black Elk recounted his vision of the world in this way:

> Then I was standing on the highest mountain of them all, and round about beneath me was the whole hoop of the world. And while I stood there, I saw more than I can tell and I understood more than I saw, for I was seeing in a sacred manner the shapes of all things in the spirit, and the shape of all shapes as they must live together like one being. And I saw that the sacred hoop of my people was one of many hoops that made one circle, wide as daylight and as a starlight, and in the center grew one mightily flowering tree to shelter all the children of one mother and one father. And I saw that it was holy.

Christ went up the mount to share his vision with the disciples and the crowds that followed him. And this is the vision he shared in what came to be called the Beatitudes:

> How blest are those who know their need of God;
> the kingdom of Heaven is theirs.
> How blest are the sorrowful;
> they shall find consolation.
> How blest are those of a gentle-spirit;
> they shall have the earth for their possession.
> How blest are those who hunger and thirst to see right prevail;
> they shall be satisfied.
> How blest are those who show mercy;
> mercy shall be shown to them.
> How blest are those whose hearts are pure;
> they shall see God.
> How blest are the peacemakers;
> God shall call them his children.
> How blest are those who are persecuted for the cause of right;
> the kingdom of Heaven is theirs. (Mt 5:3-10)

A Prayer for Vision

Shape, O Lord, our visions with your word and your life. We make this prayer through Christ our Lord, Amen.

Psalm 126: Song of the Returning Exiles

When the LORD restored the fortunes of Zion,
we came to be like those who are dreaming.
Then our mouth was filled with laughter,
and our tongues, with shouts of joy.
Then this was said among the nations:
"The LORD has done great things for these people."
The LORD has done great things for us:
we are full of joy.
Restore, O LORD, our fortunes,
as you do the torrents in the Negeb.
Those who sow in tears
will reap with joy.
When he goes forth,
the bearer of the seed to be scattered
weeps as he goes.
When he comes home,
the bearer of his own sheaves
comes shouting with joy.

Questions for Spiritual Reflection

1. What is the vision for my organization?

2. Did (does) everyone participate in creating this vision? Is it a shared vision?

3. Does this vision have everyone's commitment, especially my own?

4. What kind of vision did Jesus have for the world? Do I realistically think it is possible to shape a vision that is compatible to Jesus' vision for my organization and my life?

Chapter 8

Hope

Prayer to the Holy Spirit of Hope

O Holy Spirit, give me stillness of soul in you.
Calm the turmoil within with the gentleness of your
    peace.
Quiet the anxiety within with a deep trust in you.
Heal the wounds of sin within with the awareness of your
    presence.
Confirm the hope within with the knowledge of your
    strength.
Give fullness to the love within with an outpouring of your
    love.
O Holy Spirit, be to me a source of light, strength, and
    courage so that I may hear your call ever more
    clearly and follow it more generously. Amen.

THE SPIRITUAL LEADER INSTILLS HOPE

The spiritual dimension of leadership calls for the leader to instill hope in those who follow. People expect fulfillment. A leader must have qualities that inspire hope simply because followers aspire to become more and to achieve something. Followers hope for leaders to affirm their dignity, worth, and aspirations.

Leaders who instill hope have attainable ideals, and their behavior exemplifies their ideals in action. Followers have hope in who they are and have hope in what their organization can achieve. The leader who instills hope gives followers something to work and live for in their personal life and work. Hope needs to be felt in the face of risks, innovations, and challenges. Leaders have a mandate, especially in today's tumultuous, crisis-ridden setting, to provide people with hope for a better personal life and for meaningful work — and to do something to assure that this is the outcome.

Effective leaders rely on appeals to the hopes and ideals of their followers. Remember the story of the two bricklayers when asked what they were doing. One said, "I'm building a wall." The other replied, "I'm building a cathedral." In terms of hoped-for fulfillment for the two workers, the appeal of a grand ideal wins over the accomplishment of a simple task.

Today's world is a world desperately in need of hope. Famine and injustice plague parts of the world. In developed countries, crime and violence cause people to lose hope and to give in to cynicism and fear. Even in the U.S., where a high standard of living prevails, people are losing hope as organizations in a state of flux lay off massive numbers of workers, destroying lives and plans for the future. When members of younger generations, now building futures and starting families, are asked about their expectations, many of them show a startling loss of hope: "We don't expect to have as much as our parents did. The good jobs are leaving. People only want to employ you part-time with no benefits. We'll be lucky if we can afford a house."

Workers and whole organizations are losing hope. One defense company, which began massive layoffs in 1990, has cut 14,000 workers. Since that time, not a day has gone by when each worker was not threatened by formal or informal rumors of layoff. Says one employee,

> These are supposed to be "white collar" layoffs, but we see that those responsible for the bad management decisions — the high-earning top executives — are not being fired, but rather "quietly transferred" and even given pay raises. Our personnel department continues to blindly crank out "employee morale / corporate culture" surveys while every Friday employees wonder who will get the hatchet. The company picnic has been cancelled because no one wanted to come. The company continues to merrily endorse and spend thousands on "Total Quality" efforts, but the very foundation of the quality theories, like buy-in, communication, participation, people's dignity, and worker retraining, are nonexistent in our situation. It's a mockery. The company has a much-publicized ethics program with paid consultants from "established programs," but so often we see stories of major ethical and contract mismanagement in our local newspaper. The marketing-image phrase plastered around the organization is "A Company of Leaders," but disgruntled employees have been crossing out the 'd' in this phrase and adding a 'v,' since most people are looking for other jobs. No one wants to stay here. My wife can't wait until I find another job.

Clearly this worker describes a situation where people have lost hope, and where apparently top leaders have lost their vision for a future, and either are blind to this despair or are creating it deliberately with the intent of voluntary staff reduction. This type of corporate culture, one of desperation and lost hope, confusion, innuendo and rumor, is sadly too often the case in organizations, and perhaps it is harder than ever for leaders to provide hope in the face of tough economic times. Says one corporate CEO, "We don't have time for self-actualization or blue-sky vision statement planning. We are in a day-to-day survival mode." While these are very practical and understandable sentiments, what this CEO fails to realize is that, without hope or a vision for the future, the organization will almost certainly fail — regardless of economic and competitive conditions.

The successful business leaders that Bennis and Nanus studied (1985) sometimes even saw failure as a springboard of hope for themselves and for others. These leaders found a way to benefit from failure.

Bennis and Nanus found a fusion between positive self-regard and optimism about a desired outcome. These same successful leaders had a positive regard for others — perhaps not, as in the anecdote above, a contempt for what the workers were thinking and feeling. They were effective in making others feel good and did not criticize others until the others were convinced of the leader's unconditional confidence in their abilities. These successful leaders were found to create a sense of confidence and high expectation that fostered motivation among followers.

The faith of Christian leaders lives in hope, in the expectations of God's promises.

Hope as one of the theological virtues (faith, hope, charity) means looking forward to the next world. St. Augustine says that of the three theological virtues hope is the greatest. Faith tells us that God *is* and love tells us that God *is good*, but hope tells us that God *will work God's will*. Augustine continues: hope has two lovely daughters: anger and courage; anger so that what must not be *may not be* and courage so that what should be *can be*.

The virtue of hope can fill Christian leaders with courage to cooperate in the work of God's kingdom. By action of the Holy Spirit, hope with faith and love completes and perfects the cardinal virtues of justice, prudence, temperance, and fortitude.

What Hope Can Do:

- Hope can encourage leaders to strive for justice in their relations with others.

- Hope can instill a spiritual sense of the future, so that leaders become prudent in decisions they make.
- Hope can help leaders to practice temperance, moderation, and simplicity in using organizational resources.
- Hope can give a leader strength to practice fortitude in the face of violence and temptation.
- Hope can indeed work wonders for leaders. In turn leaders can give followers the gift and blessing of hope.

William Lynch, in *Images of Hope*, describes how hope in the future is connected with our ability to imagine. Simone Weil provides some understanding of this mystery as well. The distinction that she makes between affliction and suffering is in her essay, "The Love of God and Affliction." In *Waiting for God*, she seems to get to the heart of what Lynch is speaking about, and she expands the discussion of entrapment and of ways to escape that cycle of despair. She writes:

> It [affliction] takes possession of the soul and marks it through and through with its own particular mark, the mark of slavery.
>
> Affliction is inseparable from physical suffering and yet quite distinct. With suffering, all that is not bound up with physical pain or something analogous is artificial, imaginary, and can be eliminated by a suitable adjustment of the mind.
>
> Affliction is an uprooting of life, a more or less attenuated equivalent of death, made irresistibly present to the soul by the attack or immediate apprehension of physical pain. There is not really affliction unless there is social degradation or the fear of it in some form or another.

Affliction enslaves the soul, uproots life, and frightens. Weil and Lynch claim that to be lifted from affliction, imaging hope — the kind that provides a clear picture of a better life or better way of being — must be shared.

The Christian community is one that must hope together in

the face of suffering, evil, and death. Through our participation in the Paschal Mystery we are called to enter into the suffering and affliction of others. By entering into their affliction, we come closer to sharing in the suffering and death of Christ. To many this is sheer folly. Hope in the face of evil calls for struggle. The question about our hope is connected with the question of God's promise. Hope calls for a return to the promise delivered to the prophets of the Old Testament who were awaiting the coming of the Messiah.

Through Jeremiah, God speaks to the people exiled in Babylon:

> I know well the plans I have in mind for you, says the Lord, plans for your welfare, plans to give you a future of hope. When you call me, when you go to pray to me, I will listen to you. When you look for me, you will find me. Yes, when you seek me with all your heart, you will find me with you, says the Lord, and I will change your lot. (Jr 29:11-14)

In the New Testament we are assured of the power of hopeful prayer when Christ said:

> Ask, and you will receive. Seek, and you will find. Knock, and it will be opened to you. For the one who asks, receives. The one who seeks, finds. The one who knocks, enters. (Mt 7:7-8)

The story of *The Rabbi's Gift* demonstrates a lack of the Christian communal sense in hope of the glory of God.

> There was a famous monastery which had fallen on hard times. Formerly its many buildings were filled with young monks and its big church resounded with the singing of the chant, but now it was nearly deserted. People no longer came there to be nourished by prayer. A handful of old monks shuffled through the cloisters and praised their God with heavy hearts.
>
> On the edge of the monastery woods, an old rabbi had built a

little hut. He would come there from time to time to fast and pray. No one ever spoke with him, but whenever he appeared, the word would be passed from monk to monk: "The rabbi walks in the woods." And for as long as he was there, the monks would feel sustained by his prayerful presence.

One day the abbot decided to visit the rabbi and to open his heart to him. So after the morning Eucharist, he set out through the woods. As he approached the hut, the abbot saw the rabbi standing in the doorway, his arms outstretched in welcome. It was as though he had been waiting there for some time. The two embraced like long-lost brothers. Then they stepped back and just stood there, smiling at one another with smiles their faces could hardly contain.

After a while the rabbi motioned the abbot to enter. In the middle of the room was a wooden table with the Scriptures open on it. They sat there for a moment in the presence of the book. Then the rabbi began to cry. The abbot could not contain himself. He covered his face with his hands and began to cry, too. For the first time in his life, he cried his heart out. The two men sat there like lost children, filling the hut with their sobs and wetting the wood of the table with their tears.

After the tears had ceased to flow and all was quiet again, the rabbi lifted his head. "You and your brothers are serving God with heavy hearts," he said. "You have come to ask a teaching of me. I will give you this teaching, but you can only repeat it once. After that, no one must say it aloud again."

The rabbi looked straight at the abbot and said, "The Messiah is among you." For a while, all was silent. The rabbi said, "Now you must go." The abbot left without a word and without ever looking back.

The monks did not recognize the reign of God in their midst.

The Rabbi's Gift, like Isaiah's prophecy of Jesus as God's chosen servant, recapitulates for Christian leaders the hope of the glory of God through Jesus Christ:

Here is my servant, whom I have chosen,
the one I love, and with whom I am pleased.
I will send my Spirit upon him,
and he will announce my judgment to the nations.
He will not argue or shout,
    or make loud speeches in the streets.
He will not break off a bent reed,
    nor will he put out a flickering lamp.
He will persist until he causes justice to triumph;
    and all peoples will put their hope in him. (Is 42:1-4)

By placing their hope in Christ, even in the face of — or perhaps especially in the face of — difficult, challenging times, leaders can mirror their intimate union with God in their words and actions. They can be persistent in leading truth to victory, in leading followers to put their hope in Christ.

Christian leaders can pray and "ask the God of our Lord Jesus Christ to give [them] a spirit of wisdom and revelation by which [they'll] come to a knowledge of him… and come to know what the hope is to which He calls [them], how rich is His glorious heritage which will be shared among the saints, and how extraordinary is His great power in [those] who believe" (Eph 1:18-19).

Leaders can foster a spirit of hope in themselves and in their followers and can grasp something of the mystery hidden for ages and generations: God's will is that all be saved. The working out of this mystery is something that we "wait for with patience" (Rm 8:24-25) and with hope. We know that God, the source of hope, will fill us all with joy and peace through our belief in him, so that we will overflow with hope by the power of the Holy Spirit (cf. Rm 15:13).

In instilling hope in followers, leaders can heed these words of Paul in his First Letter to the Thessalonians:

You yourselves are well aware that the Day of the Lord will come like a thief in the night… We must be clothed in the breastplate of faith and love and the helmet of hope in salva-

tion through our Lord Jesus Christ. So encourage and
strengthen one another, just as you are doing. (1 Th 5:2, 11)

A Prayer to the God of Hope

Life's most difficult times seem the most hopeless, but this is
precisely when people need to pray for hope. When you are feeling a loss of hope, take a quiet moment to reflect and pray to the
God of Hope. A Psalm of Praise follows.

Holy God, light our hearts with your *hope,* to give us strength
always to do your will. We make this prayer through Christ our
Lord. Amen.

Psalm 33: Joyful Song to the Creator

Shout joyfully, you righteous, on account of the LORD.
It behooves the upright to give praise.
Give thanks to the LORD on the lyre.
Sing psalms to him on the psaltery of ten strings.
Sing a new song to him;
play the harp skillfully amid shouts of triumph.
For the word of the LORD is upright,
and all his works subsist on faithfulness.
He loves righteousness and justice;
the earth is full of the LORD's loving kindness.
The heavens were made through the word of the LORD;
and all their host, through the breath of his mouth.
He heaps up the waters of the sea as in a mound;
in storerooms he lays up the surges of the deep.
Keep away from the LORD in fear, all the earth.
Stay away from him in awe, you inhabitants of the world.
For he spoke, and it came to be;
he commanded, and it stood at attention.
The LORD foils the plans of nations;
he frustrates the designs of peoples.
The LORD's plan stands forever;
the designs of his mind, from generation to generation.

Happy the nation whose God is the LORD;
happy the people he has chosen for his inheritance.
The LORD observes from heaven;
he watches the whole human race.
From his dwelling-place he gazes
upon all earth's inhabitants
— he who forms their hearts, all of them,
who discerns all their deeds.
There is no king who is saved by a great army;
no valiant warrior who is delivered by great might.
As for safety, the horse is a disappointment;
for all its strength, it cannot provide escape.
Look! The LORD's eye is on those who fear him,
directed toward those who wait for his loving kindness
so as to deliver their souls from death,
and keep them alive in famine.
Our soul has waited for the LORD,
who is our help and our shield,
for it is in him that our heart rejoices,
it is in his holy name that we have trusted.
O LORD, may your loving kindness be upon us
even as we have placed our hope in you.

Questions for Spiritual Reflection

1. What hope do I have for the future? What images does my hope embody?

2. How do I give hope to others?

3. What hope does Christ's message and example offer to me?

Chapter 9

Integrity

This is what Yahweh asks
of you; only this:

To act justly,
to love tenderly, and
to walk humbly with your God. (Micah 6:8)

Prayer to the Holy Spirit of Integrity

Come, Holy Spirit, fill the hearts of your faithful,
And kindle in them the fire of your love.
Send forth your spirit, O Lord, and renew the face of the
     earth.

O God, on the first Pentecost
You instructed the hearts of those who believed in you
by the light of the Holy Spirit.

Under the inspiration of the same Spirit, give us a
taste for what is right and true and a continuing
sense of the Spirit's joy-bringing presence and power,
Through Jesus Christ our Lord. Amen.

If I speak with the tongues of angels,
but have not love,
my words are but a clanging cymbal,
a discordant harp. (1 Cor 13:1)

THE SPIRITUAL LEADER HAS INTEGRITY

The spiritual side of leadership demands integrity in the leader. A leader of integrity is an honest person who lives by a personal and professional ethical code. A leader of integrity sets fire to others' hearts by exemplifying wholeness in the personal and professional dimensions of daily life. According to the philosopher Aristotle, a leader of integrity is a person of virtue.

In any organization, members are expected not only to do their jobs, but to do them honestly. The expectation is that the work will be done well and with a sense of integrity. Subordinates want managers to be thoughtful and helpful; managers want subordinates to be loyal and cooperative. Both want people of integrity and honor.

Authenticity in relations is particularly binding for professionals who are guided by codes of morality — and professional character is at the core of these codes. The value that various professions place on the integrity and character of their practitioners is reflected in codes.

Karen Lebacqz, in *Professional Ethics: Power and Paradox*, argues that trustworthiness is the underlying theme of qualities expected of professionals through professional codes. A professional leader of integrity is trustworthy because that person is honest, fair, helpful, and not hurtful. The ethics of character and action are complementary. A person of integrity is truthful and tells the truth. A person of integrity is just and acts justly. A person of integrity is caring and cares for others.

Concern for integrity began long before it was identified among the leaders in "The 10 Best Companies" studied by Peters and Waterman or the CEOs studied by Bennis and Nanus. Lao Tzu, the great Chinese sage of the 6th century BC, wrote about "The Leader's Integrity," in *Tao Te Ching*:

> The wise leader knows that the true nature of events cannot be captured in words. So why pretend? Confusing jargon is one sign of a leader who does not know how things happen.
>
> But what cannot be said can be demonstrated: be silent, be

conscious. Consciousness works. It sheds light on what is happening. It clarifies conflicts and harmonizes the agitated individual or group field. [T]he group field is when nothing is happening in the group or it is the silences or empty spaces that reveal the group's essential mood, the context for everything that happens.

The leader also knows that all existence is a single whole. Therefore the leader is a neutral observer who takes no sides.

The leader cannot be seduced by offers or threats. Money, love, or fame, whether gained or lost, do not sway the leader from the center.

The leader's integrity is not idealistic. It rests on a pragmatic knowledge of how things work.

In summary, Lao Tzu's leader of integrity communicates clearly and openly, listens, and is impartial, committed to the center, and realistic. This leader will "know how things happen" and will act accordingly.

Stephen Covey, in his much acclaimed book, *The Seven Habits of Highly Effective People*, says that in proving integrity and character, actions speak louder than words. "What we *are* communicates far more eloquently than anything we *say* or *do*. There are people we trust because we know their character. Whether they're eloquent or not, whether they have human-relations techniques or not, we trust them and work successfully with them."

Integrity thus seems to be something of who we are and something that we live. It seems to be a set of virtues and habits that we learn from personal and professional life. In their article, "Ethics in the Education of Business Managers," Charles Power and David Vogel state that:

> We doubt that personal integrity can be taught in any simple sense; we similarly doubt that managerial integrity can be simply taught. But we do believe that there are teachable tools, skills, and capabilities that will help in the development of managers who understand what an ethical decision requires

in the light of personal commitments, the organizational ethos
and purpose, and the social context in which the organization
lives and plays its role.

Kenneth Blanchard and Norman Vincent Peale, co-authors of an
inspiring and practical book, *The Power of Ethical Management*,
describe a number of tools and skills that can be used in teaching
ethics in business. They demonstrate through cases, stories, and
sound philosophical-spiritual models why integrity pays and why
ethical decision-making is effective. Business leaders with a sense
of integrity and fair play help to create a healthy work environment
where people do not have to cheat to win.

In approaching ethical decisions, Blanchard and Peale suggest that a leader ask three questions:

1. Is it legal?	Will I be violating either civil law or company policy?
2. Is it balanced?	Is it fair to all concerned in the short term as well as in the long term? Does it promote win-win relationships?
3. How will it make me feel about myself?	Will it make me proud? Would I feel good if my decision was published in the newspaper? Would I feel good if my family knew about it?

Blanchard and Peale advance five core principles of ethical power
for people and organizations to ensure genuine, lasting fulfillment
in personal and organizational life. The five principles summarized
in Table 4 are: Purpose, Pride, Patience, Persistence, and Perspective. In learning the five P's, Blanchard and Peale say that patience
and pride are the most difficult. They counsel that everything won't
happen "yesterday and don't let pride get in the way of your
changes."

Experts on integrity seem to indicate that this virtue is really
a constellation of qualities: honesty, fairness, openness, loyalty. It
also seems that these qualities can be taught but are more easily

Table 4

An adaptation of Blanchard and Peale's five core principles of ethical power for persons and organizations to foster ethical decision-making and good performance.

	INDIVIDUALS	ORGANIZATIONAL LEADERS
1. Purpose	• Behave in a way that makes you feel good about yourself • Live a personal mission statement that assures you of being an ethical person	• Communicate a mission of the organization throughout the organization • Guide with values, hopes and a vision that will assure acceptable behavior
2. Pride	• Feel good about your accomplishments •Temper pride with healthy self-esteem and humility	• Maintain integrity in the organization by helping employ-ees to feel good about themselves and the company • Catch people doing the right things and praise them • Care for your employees
3. Patience	• Believe that no matter what happens, things will turn out right, if you believe in some-thing greater than yourself: God, spirituality, a higher power	• Trust that your values and beliefs are right over the long term • Get all employees to invest energy and adhere to the overall purpose, policies, and procedures of the organization
4. Persistence	• Be committed to behaving ethically at all times • Act consistently with your guiding principles	• Believe in yourself, your product/service and the organization • Be consistent in adhering to established ethical standards and vision
5. Perspective	• See what is important in any situation • Balance your external self (your task oriented side) with your inner self (your reflective and thoughtful side) • Wake up your inner self to facilitate problem-solving and to put things in perspective by quiet time: prayer, devotional reading, music, bicycling, etc.	• Assess and reflect on where the organization is, where it is going, and how it is going to get there • Take time for strategic planning, reflecting and involving people before making any final decision • Aim to balance planning and implementation, reflection and action

"caught" through exemplary role modelling, monitoring, and coaching by moral leaders or mentors.

In the final analysis, integrity seems to stem from the soul. Remember the thought-provoking parable of the lost soul in the Introduction? The soul is the resting place for values, purpose in life, and the kind of person one wants to be. Good ethical behavior comes from the soul. And it is up to the organization's leaders to ensure that the organizational soul retains its values and ethics.

Christian leaders likewise are entrusted not only by society, but also by God. As Christians we are expected to be Christ-like. What we do needs to be based on what we are — followers of Christ. The only true means to integrity is to base one's life on the moral authority of the Gospel with all that such a commitment implies.

Christ came into the world to bear witness to the truth (Jn 18:37). He became one of us (Ph 2:7) and worked among the hungry, the thirsty, the alienated, the naked, the sick, and the imprisoned. Christ's love extended to prostitutes, lepers and tax collectors.

Following Christ as proposed by the Gospel is authentic Christian leadership. Christian leaders must see their work and role truly as a ministry, and through their ministerial life they must treat others with dignity and love, not moral superiority or self-righteousness. They take action to manifest God's justice, love, joy, and peace. They bring good news to the poor, liberty to prisoners, new sight to the blind, freedom to the oppressed (cf. Lk 4:18-19). They call unloving and unjust systems into question.

In the late 1980s, Bill Moyers did a series for public television called "A World of Ideas." This series portrayed conversations with a number of women and men about life in America and about ideas that will be shaping its future. The late historian Barbara Tuchman made some thought-provoking comments on crises she saw facing America in moving into the last decade of the twentieth century and beyond. She remarked:

What's happened is the disappearance of a positive goal. The
public as a whole is not concerned with solving the problems
of the poor, of the homeless, though they should be, because
these ultimately can be dangerous to everyone's ordinary life.
But something more seems to me to have happened, and that
is the loss of a moral sense, of knowing the difference between
right and wrong, and of being governed by it.

Tuchman defined exactly what she meant by moral sense: "The
sense of what is inherently right and wrong, and of following your
belief in what is right."

Honor, integrity, courage, and heroism seem lost in our culture today. Earlier on public television, Bill Moyers interviewed
the late Joseph Campbell in a series entitled, "The Power of Myth."
There seems to be a correlation between the moral lassitude plagu-
ing our society and a dearth of truly great moral heroes. We have
become a society whose only heroes are sports and rock stars,
people who are not known for being bearers of any kind of moral
standard. Campbell said that there are two types of heroic deeds.
"One is a physical deed, in which the hero performs a courageous
act in battle or saves a life. The other kind is a spiritual deed, in
which the hero learns to experience the supernormal range of human spiritual life and then comes back with a message."

Campbell commented on the structure of the spiritual sense
of the heroic venture. He said that "it can be seen in the puberty or
initiation rituals of early tribal societies, through which a child is
compelled to give up its childhood and become an adult: to die,
you might say, to its infantile personality and psyche and come back
as a responsible adult. This is a fundamental psychological transformation that everyone has to undergo. To evolve out of this position of psychological immaturity to the courage of self-responsi-
bility and assurance requires a death and a resurrection. That's the
basic motif of the universal hero's journey leaving one condition
and finding the source of life to bring you forth into a richer or
mature condition."

The Paschal Mystery: the life, death, and resurrection of Jesus

Christ can be viewed from this perspective. Christians are called and challenged to pattern their lives on Christ's life, death, and rising. That is the heroic venture. That is the venture to which Christian leaders are called. It can take a very dramatic manifestation, which can inspire all of us to follow Christ, hero and leader.

Throughout the history of Christianity there have been people willing to live their lives by dying to self in imitation of Christ. Even in modern times, there are men and women who embody the kind of moral courage and integrity that defines true heroism. In November of 1989 six Jesuit priests were dragged from their beds in a dormitory at the José San Simeon-Canas University of Central America in San Salvador, the capital of El Salvador. They, with their housekeeper and her daughter, were shot with high-powered rifles. Back in 1980, Archbishop Oscar Romero was killed while saying Mass in a hospital chapel. Later in that year, four American churchwomen were brutally murdered in El Salvador. One of the sisters killed, Maryknoll Sister Maura Clarke, wrote a letter several months before her death, commenting on the Archbishop's martyrdom. She wrote:

> Archbishop Romero and all the martyrs of this little violent land must be interceding for a new day for Salvador. I am beginning to see death in a new way. For all these precious men, women, and children struggling in just laying down their lives as victims, it is surely a passageway to life — or better, a change of life.
>
> I don't know what tomorrow will bring. I am at peace here and searching, trying to learn what the Lord is asking. At this point, I would hope to be able to go on, God willing — This seems to be what I'm being asked to do now. The work is really what Archbishop Romero called "*acompanamiento*" (accompanying the people), as well as searching for ways to bring help. Keep us in your heart and prayers, especially the poor forsaken people.
>
> Love, Maura.

Somehow we are all affected, every human being is diminished,

when some of our brothers and sisters are tortured and killed for
having the moral integrity and courage to follow Christ's spirit of
leadership. These were people imbued with the spirit of peace and
justice and truth. They were willing to live their lives in fidelity to
that spirit. They are heirs of Christ — heroes. Jesus said once:

> Nation will rise against nation, but before any of this, they
> will manhandle and persecute you all because of my name.
> And you will be delivered up even by your parents, brothers,
> relatives, and friends. And some of you will be put to death.
> All will hate you because of me. Yet not a hair of your head
> will be harmed. By patient endurance you will save your lives.
> (Lk 21:10-19)

In their search for truth in today's world and society, Jesus says to
Christian leaders as he said to the Jews who believed in him:

> If you abide in my word,
> you're truly disciples of mine,
> and you will know the truth
> and the truth will set you free. (Jn 8:31-32)

The ultimate truth for leaders of integrity is their love for God. "This
is what love is: not that we loved God, but that He loved us" (1 Jn
4:10). In search of discovering God's love and believing that "He
lived among us" (Jn 1:14), Christian leaders learn that Jesus emp-
tied and humbled himself to give witness to God's truth. In the face
of evils like oppression, dominance, exploitation, racial injustice,
violence, and violation of human rights, Christian leaders of integrity are challenged to give witness to God's truth as Christ did. The
spirit of Christ's leadership is the truth that made him free. The same
Holy Spirit guards and guides leaders of integrity as brothers and
sisters of Christ, sons and daughters of God the Father. And when
the Spirit of truth comes to them, they will be led to the complete
truth (Jn 16:7-14).

Integrity or authentic human living is centered in God and on

God. Jesus said, "It is not those who say to me, 'Lord, Lord,' who will enter the kingdom of heaven, but those who do the will of my Father in heaven" (Mt 7:21). Discerning God's will demands a life of prayer in order to find peace with God and from God. This accountability to God will be rewarded accordingly, as indicated by Christ's description of the Last Judgment:

> When the Son of Man comes in his glory, with all his angels with him, he'll sit on the throne of his glory... Then the king will say to those at his right hand, "Come, you blessed of my Father, receive the Kingdom prepared for you from the foundation of the world. For I was hungry and you gave me to eat; I was thirsty and you gave me to drink; I was a stranger and you took me in; naked and you clothed me; I was sick and you cared for me; I was in prison and you came to see me." Then the righteous will say to him in reply, "Lord, when did we see you hungry and feed you; or thirsty and give you to drink? When did we see you a stranger and take you in; naked and clothe you; When did we see you sick or in prison and come to you?" And in answer the King will say to them, "Amen, I say to you, insofar as you did it for one of these least of my brothers, you did it for me." And the righteous [will go off] to eternal life." (Mt 25:31, 34-40, 46)

A Prayer for Integrity

Infinite Love, cleanse our hearts so that we may lead others to you with *integrity* and joy. We make this prayer through Christ our Lord. Amen.

Psalm 101: For Integrity

I will sing of loving kindness and righteousness.
To you, LORD, will I sing psalms.
I will apply my mind to the pursuit of integrity.
When will it come to me!
I will conduct myself with an upright heart

among my own.
I will never have an eye
for anything evil;
I hate evildoing,
it will never fasten upon me.
Hearts that are crooked shall part company with me;
I will have no acquaintance with evil.
I will get rid of anyone
who slanders his neighbor secretly;
I will never pair up with someone
of haughty eyes and insolent heart.
I keep my eyes on the reliable of the land
that they may live with me;
he who follows the way of integrity
— he will be in attendance upon me.
No one who acts deceitfully
shall live among my own;
no one who tells lies
shall stand in my presence.
Every morning I will put away the wicked in the land
so as to rid the city of the LORD of all wrongdoers.

Questions for Spiritual Reflection

1. Do I have integrity?
2. Who are my heroes?
3. How do I approach ethical decisions?

Chapter 10

Prayerfulness

From the riches of His glory, [may God] grant you inner strength and power through His Spirit. May Christ dwell in your hearts through faith, firmly rooted and established in love, so that with all the saints you may be able to understand the breadth, the length, the height, and the depth, and know Christ's love which surpasses all knowledge so that you may be filled with all God's fullness. (Eph 3:16-19)

A Prayer for Transformation

Let every word be the fruit of action
and reflection.
Reflection alone without action
or tending towards it
is mere theory
adding its weight
when we are overloaded
with it already
and it has led the young to despair.

Action alone without reflection
is being busy pointlessly.
Honor the Word eternal
and speak to make

a new world possible.

— Helder Camara, *The Desert is Fertile*,
London: Sheed and Ward, 1971, pp. 58-59.

THE PROCESS OF TRANSFORMATIONAL
LEADERSHIP AND PRAYING

In previous chapters we talked about the need for renewal through prayer and turning inward. It is essential that people renew their own hearts before attempting to transform anything external. But reflection without action becomes mere navel-gazing. Words without deeds are as clanging cymbals. After inward renewal, prayer and visioning, it is time for true transformation — for leaders to turn outward and take action to become organizational and social change agents. But what is meant by transformational leadership?

Leadership as a process can be understood through study and application of James MacGregor Burns's model of leadership, described as:

> a stream of evolving relationships or inter-relationships in which leaders are continuously evoking motivational responses from followers and modifying their behavior as they meet responsiveness or resistance, in a ceaseless process of flow and counterflow. (*Leadership*, p. 440)

Burns's theory is based on an understanding of the nature of power, i.e. the relation between power-holders and recipients of power. The use of power is viewed as a collective act, and involves the motives and resources of power-holders and recipients, shared goals, and the relations among all these elements.

Leaders are expected to recognize and achieve goals that are held mutually by leaders and followers. Their relation centers on the shared goals, and can result in two forms of leadership: transactional and transformational leadership. We have illustrated the interactive relations among the major concepts of Burns's theory in Table 5 below:

Table 5

The Powers	Goals	Leadership Style
Power Holder/Leader (Motives & Resources)		Transactional Leadership
	Relations (Shared Goals)	
Power Recipient/ Follower		Transformational Leadership

Transactional leadership is characterized by leaders' making contacts to exchange economic, political, or psycho-social goods. Activities may include building coalitions, setting agendas, being visible when things go wrong, or being invisible when things go right. It means listening, encouraging, and being tough if necessary.

The transactional leader motivates followers by appealing to lower needs of self-interest. Supervisors pay or promote subordinates based on their efforts or other contributions to the organization. Politicians exchange contracts or positions for votes and campaign contributions. Ideally transactional leaders engage in exchanges that involve honesty, fairness, responsibility, and reciprocity.

In contrast, transformational leadership is a less frequent form of leadership. It is a process by which "leaders and followers seek to raise one another to higher levels of morality and motivation." The consciousness and conduct of followers are raised by leaders appealing to ideals and moral values such as freedom, justice, equality, peace, and humanitarianism.

Transforming leaders and followers transcend daily responsibilities, unite purpose, and link power bases. This form of leadership leads to creating or renewing institutional purpose, shaping visions and values, and making the mission a living reality for all members of the organization. For the transforming leader no opportunity is too small, no forum too insignificant, no group too junior, no system or institution too tight to work with in achieving these high aspirations.

The process of transformational leadership is not absolutely clear. Transformational leadership and charismatic leadership are often used interchangeably. In his book *Leadership and Performance Beyond Expectations*, B.M. Bass states that "charisma is a necessary ingredient of transformational leadership, but by itself is not sufficient to account for the transformational process." In addition, Bass contends that transactional and transformational leadership, though distinct, are not mutually exclusive. Leaders may use both types of leadership in different situations. Bass believes also that transformational leadership can take negative or positive forms. Gandhi, Florence Nightingale, and founders of religious communities (such as Catherine MacAuley and Ignatius of Loyola), and countless other reformers were positive transformational leaders. Ruthless leaders such as Adolf Hitler, Catherine the Great, and drug lords are examples of negative transformational leaders — leaders who acted out of the shadow side of leadership.

The initiatives of Mikhail Gorbachev as president of the Soviet Union were an example of transformational leadership in progress. He introduced the strategies of "*glasnost*" and "*perestroika*" to uproot Communist culture. His challenge was to transform communistic assumptions, values, beliefs, and perceptions to democratic ones. His task was to raise people's consciousness to see that some of the basic values of the Communist state are unjust or obsolete. To some degree, Gorbachev was successful in that he was able to uproot Communist culture at the expense of his own position as leader. The group of nations that were once the Soviet Union now are grappling with the transformation begun by Gorbachev, and it is uncertain that a new way of life based on justice and freedom will be achieved. But the amazing and tremendous change and decline of the rule of Communism in the former Soviet Union attest to the power of transformational leadership. Only time will tell whether negative or positive transformational leadership will prevail there.

There are many transactional Christian leaders today: presidents, principals, provincials, shop stewards, supervisors, CEO's, and captains. Transactional leaders may be involved in social justice programs: setting up soup kitchens and shelters, counseling alcoholics and drug addicts, volunteering for hospice and senior citizens' programs, planning educational or liturgical programs, lobbying against unfair housing or for healthcare reform.

Transforming the leadership of a Christian leader goes beyond being employed or ministering in small or large public or private corporations, or even in social justice programs. It is recognizing the call of Christ to the ways of his Gospel. It is going aside, as Christ did, to spend time with God to listen to God's Spirit and learn from that (cf. Jn 14:26, 16:8). It is taking time to let the Spirit of God set one's own heart on fire before going out as a leader to transform and set the world on fire.

Through prayerful listening, the Holy Spirit can raise leaders and followers to new heights of motivation and morality. Each asks: "What must I do to be saved?" This kind of spirituality is based on Christ's own spirituality. As Christ said, "For I haven't spoken on my own; it's the Father Who sent me Who has Himself commanded me what to say and what to speak. And I know that His commands mean eternal life" (Jn 12:49-50).

Christian leaders are called to a level of transformational leadership that can be achieved only through a prayer life. Through the Spirit of God given to them in prayer, they can be anointed and sent like Christ "to bring the good news to the poor..., to proclaim release to captives and recovery of sight to the blind, to set at liberty the oppressed, to proclaim the acceptable year of the Lord" (Lk 4:18-19).

Christian transforming leaders experience Christ and recognize that unless the "Lord builds a house," teaches a course, develops a project, they "labor in vain." They also believe that "unless the Lord watches over the city," presides over a corporation or board, supervises a kitchen or a shelter, they supervise in vain.

The transforming Christian leader involved in a busy apostolic life, confronting oppressive systems, and ministering the spiritual and corporal works of mercy may experience what Christ did after the miracle of the loaves and fishes and the walk on the water. Persons may not get into boats "and [cross] to Capernaum to look for Jesus" (Jn 6:24) but they may find all kinds of ways to get more from their time, energy, and talents. These Christian leaders need to be mindful that their influence as transforming leaders must transcend the apostolic work itself as indicated by Christ's words to those assembled in the synagogue at Capernaum:

> "Amen, amen, I say to you,
> you seek me not because you saw signs
> but because you ate of the loaves and were satisfied.
> Labor not for food that perishes,
> but for food that remains for life eternal,
> which the Son of Man will give you,
> for God the Father has set His seal on him." (Jn 6:27)

Transforming Christian leaders are strengthened by partaking of Christ's flesh and blood. Some of the most profound expressions of Christ's prayer and transforming leadership centered on his breaking bread with others. The Holy Spirit sent by the Father was present when Christ "took the five loaves and the two fish and, looking up to heaven, gave a blessing" (Mt 14:19). On a second occasion, Christ "took the [seven] loaves and the fish and gave thanks, and he broke them and kept giving them to his disciples, and the disciples gave them to the crowds." Through the power of Christ's prayer, "They all ate and were filled" (Mt 15:36-37). Like Christ, whatever transforming leaders eat, whatever they drink, whatever they do, they do it for the glory of God, that all may be saved (1 Cor 10:31).

The spirit of Christ's transforming leadership was memorialized when on the night before he met death, he sat at the table with those he loved and "took some bread, blessed it, broke it, and gave it to them, saying, 'This is my body which is given up for you; do this in memory of me'" (Lk 22:19).

In the celebration of the Eucharist, Christian leaders and followers offer the life-giving bread and saving cup in memory of Christ's death and resurrection. They proclaim "Christ has died, Christ is risen, Christ will come again." They pray that this sacrifice of thanksgiving will lead them to the eternal praise of God. In commemorating Christ's sacrifice, leaders and followers are transformed to be ever-watchful in prayer, strong in love, and faithful to the breaking of the bread in every human experience and act, no matter how commonplace or lofty.

Pierre Teilhard de Chardin talks about this transformation in his work, *The Divine Milieu*:

> In our hands, in the hands of all of us, the world and life (our world, our life) are placed like a Host, ready to be charged with the divine influence, that is to say with a real Presence of the Incarnate Word. The mystery will be accomplished. But on one condition: which is that we shall believe that this has the will and the power to become for us the action — *that is to say the prolongation* — of the Body of Christ. If we believe, then everything is illuminated and takes shape around us: chance is seen to be order, success assumes an incorruptible plenitude, suffering becomes a visit and a caress of God. (pp. 116-117)

As with the two on the road to Emmaus, something may prevent transactional leaders from recognizing the Risen Lord in themselves and others. The potential of these leaders for transforming leadership can be realized through prayer. The apostles reached new heights of understanding, faith, and love when they realized Christ stayed with them in prayer. "And it happened that when he reclined at table with them, he took the bread and blessed it, broke it, and gave it to them. Then their eyes were opened and they recognized him ... in the breaking of the bread" (Lk 24:30-35).

Like the disciples on the way to Emmaus, transactional Christian leaders can convert to transformational Christian leadership. Regardless of the organizational setting, all leaders need to allow the Holy Spirit to work within them through prayer. Leaders need to discern God's life-giving Spirit among themselves and in followers. Through prayer, the Holy Spirit can work through Christian leaders to transform oppression to empowerment, isolation to solidarity, injustice to justice, sorrow to joy, hate to love. Through the healing power of the Holy Spirit, leaders and followers are transformed, brought together as sisters and brothers of Christ, sons and daughters of God. The Kingdom of God in any organizational setting "consists of righteousness, peace and joy in the Holy Spirit" (Rm 14:17).

Blessings and transformation will continue for leaders as they continually praise God. By discerning and meeting the Spirit of truth in prayer, transforming leaders and followers reach new heights of leadership and empowerment, in attitudes, dialogue, emotional wisdom, renewal, in shaping visions, hope, integrity, and prayer.

A Prayer for Transformation

Powerful God, transform us through our *prayers*. Help us to seek you and to live and lead others in your love. We ask this through Christ our Lord. Amen.

Psalm 63: Ardent Longing for God

O God, you are my God. For you am I searching.
In a scorching, exhausted land without water
my soul thirsts for you,
for you my flesh languishes.
This is how I used to contemplate you in the sanctuary,
admiring your strength and your splendor.
Since your loving kindness is more enjoyable than life,
my lips want to praise you.
Thus do I want to bless you throughout my life,
to raise my hands for the sake of your name.
My soul will have its fill as if of marrow and fat,
and my mouth will extol you with joyful lips.
Since I remember you on my bed,

I will meditate on you through hours of the night.
Since you have become a helper for me,
I will shout joyfully in the shelter of your wings.
My soul is deeply attached to you;
your right hand sustains me.
But as regards those who seek my life to destroy it,
let them sink into the lowest parts of the earth;
let them be handed over to the sword,
and become the jackals' share.
Let the king, instead, rejoice in God,
let all those boast who swear by Him;
for the mouth of those will be stopped who speak to deceive.

Questions for Spiritual Reflection

1. Is my leadership style transformational or transactional?

2. If transactional, can I "transform to transformational" through prayer?

3. Christ's Gospel calls me to transform oppressive structures. Where do I start in my own organization?

Prayer to God, The Holy Spirit

Come, true light,
Come, eternal life,
Come, secret of hiddenness.
Come, delight that has no name.
Come, unutterableness.
Come, O presence, forever fleeing from human nature.
Come, everlasting jubilee.
Come, light without end.
Come, awaited by all who are in want.
Come, resurrection of the dead.
Come, mighty one, forever creating,
    recreating and renewing with a mere wave of Thy hand.
Come, Thou who remainest wholly invisible,
    for none ever to grasp or to caress.
Come, Thou who flowest in the river of hours,
    yet immovable stayest above it,
    who dwellest above all heavens,
    yet bendest to us who are bowed down.
Come, most longed-for and most hallowed name:
    to express what Thou art,
    to comprehend how Thou art,
    is forever denied to us.
Come, perpetual joy.
Come, unwitherable wreath.
Come, O purple raiment of Our Lord and God.
Come, girdle, clear as crystal and many-colored with precious
    gems.
Come, inaccessible refuge.
Come, Thou whom my poor soul desireth and hath desired.
Come, lonely one, to the lonely one,
    for lonely I am, as Thou canst see.
Come, Thou who hast made me solitary and forlorn on earth.
Come, Thou who hast become my longing,
    for that Thou hast ordained that I must needs long for Thee
    whom no human breath has ever reached.
Come, my breath and my life.

Come, joy, glory, and my incessant delight.
I give Thee thanks that
   without merging or losing Thyself in my nature,
   Thou art yet one spirit with me,
And while Thou remainst God, high above everything,
Thou hast become everything to me.
Ineffable nourishment, never to be withdrawn,
   pouring forth unceasingly into the lips of my spirit
   and aboundingly filling my inner self!
I give Thee thanks that Thou hast become for me
   a day without evening
   and a sun without setting.
Thou, who hast no place to hide,
   as Thou fillest the universe with Thy power.
Never hast Thou hidden from anyone;
   we, however, hide from Thee always,
   if we dare not appear before Thy face.
And where also shouldst Thou hide,
   who hast nowhere a place to rest?
Or why shouldst Thou hide, who dost not shrink
   or shy away from anything in all the world?
Ah, Holy Land, make an abode in me,
   dwell in me, and till my departure leave me not,
   leave not Thy servant;
Then I, too, may find myself after death in Thee,
   and reign with Thee, O God, who reignest over everything.
Remain with me, Lord, do not forsake me.

Strengthen me interiorly
   that I may be unmoved at all times,
   and protect me by dwelling within me:
   that although dead, I may continue contemplating Thee,
   although poor, may be in possession of Thee.
Thus I shall be mightier than all kings:
Eating and drinking Thee
   and at chosen hours wrapping myself in Thee
   I shall enjoy unspeakable bliss.

For Thou art all Good,

all Beauty, all Beatitude
and Thine is the glory of the universe,
Thine, the Father and the Son forever and ever. Amen.

— Symeon the New Theologian

BIBLIOGRAPHY

For those interested in exploring the issue of spirituality and leadership more deeply, the authors suggest the following resources.

Adams, John D., ed., *Transforming Leadership*. Alexandria, VA: Miles River Press, 1986.

Adams, John D., ed., *Transforming Work*. Alexandria, VA: Miles River Press, 1984.

Corrado, Dennis M., and Hinchey, James F., *Shepherds Speak: American Bishops Confront the Social and Moral Issues That Challenge Christians Today*. New York: Crossroad, 1986.

Douglass, R. Bruce, ed., *The Deeper Meaning of Economic Life*. Washington, DC: Georgetown University Press, 1986.

Freeman, R. Edward, and Gilbert, Daniel R., Jr. *Corporate Strategy and the Search for Ethics*. New York: Prentice-Hall, 1988. (Good general resource on integrating ethics into corporate organizations.)

Greenleaf, Robert K., *Servant Leadership*. New York: Paulist Press, 1980.

Hall, Brian P., *The Genesis Effect: Personal and Organizational Transformations*. New York: Paulist Press, 1986.

Hall, Brian P., *Leadership Through Values: A Study in Personal and Organizational Development*. New York: Paulist Press, 1980.

Harrison, Roger, *Organization Culture and Quality of Service: A Strategy for Releasing Love in the Workplace*. Berkeley, CA: Harrison Associates, 1986.

Haughey, John C. *Converting 9 to 5: A Spirituality of Work*. New York: Crossroad, 1989. (This compelling book analyzes the spiritual importance, dignity, and meaning of work in daily life.)

Hehminiak, Daniel A., *Spiritual Development: An Interdisciplinary Study*. Chicago: Loyola University Press, 1987.

Hug, James, *Tracing the Spirit: Communities, Social Action, and Theological Reflection*. New York: Paulist Press, 1983.

Kilmann, Ralph H., *Beyond the Quick Fix*. San Francisco: Jossey-Bass, 1985. (Discusses managing organizational change with ongoing processes rather than reactionary strategies.)

Kinast, Robert, *Caring for Society: A Theological Interpretation of Lay Ministry*. Chicago: Thomas More Press, 1985.

Owen, Harrison, *Spirit-Transformation and Development in Organizations*. Potomac, MD: Abbott Publishing, 1987.

Peters, Thomas, and Waterman, Robert, "Studies in Excellence," *Director*. April 1983, pp. 44-45.

Puls, Joan, *A Spirituality of Compassion*. Mystic, CT: Twenty-Third Publications, 1988.

Shea, John, *The Spirit Master*, Chicago: Thomas More Press, 1987.

Shea, John, *An Experience Named Spirit*. Chicago: Thomas More Press, 1983.

Tichy, Noel M., and DeVanna, Mary Anne, *The Transformational Leader*. New York: John Wiley & Sons, 1986.

Weisbord, Marvin, *Productive Workplaces: Organizing and Managing for Dignity, Meaning, and Community*. San Francisco, CA: Jossey-Bass, 1987.